# British Economic Opinion: A Survey of A Thousand Economists

**MARTIN RICKETTS**
and
**EDWARD SHOESMITH**
*University of Buckingham*

*With a Preface by*
**SAMUEL BRITTAN**
*Assistant Editor,*
*Financial Times*

Published by
INSTITUTE OF ECONOMIC AFFAIRS
1990

First published in May 1990 by

The Institute of Economic Affairs,
2 Lord North Street,
Westminster, London SW1P 3LB

*Research Monograph 45*

ISSN 0073-9103
ISBN 0-255 36233-1


*The Institute gratefully acknowledges financial support for its
publications programme and other work from a generous benefaction
by the late Alec and Beryl Warren.*



Printed in Great Britain by
Goron Pro-Print Co. Ltd.,
Churchill Industrial Estate, Lancing, W. Sussex

Filmset in 'Berthold' Univers 9 on 11pt Medium

# Contents

3

# Foreword

The object of this unique IEA survey, *British Economic Opinion: A Survey of a Thousand Economists*, was to measure the degree of agreement or disagreement amongst British economists and to find out if there has been a significant change of opinion among economists about the merits of state intervention in the economy in the light of having a government committed to the ideology of a free market over the past decade.

The only previous attempt to find this out was undertaken by Samuel Brittan (1973)[1] who makes some interesting comparisons between the two surveys in his Preface.

To put this IEA survey in perspective, readers should recall that on 29 March 1981, Professor Frank Hahn and his colleagues from the Faculty of Economics and Politics, University of Cambridge, produced their infamous 'Statement on Economic Policy' which had been signed by 364 university economists in Britain and was subsequently published by *The Times*.

The statement's 'central message' was:

'We, who are all present or retired members of the economic staff of British universities, are concerned that:

(a) there is no basis in economic theory or supporting evidence for the Government's belief that by deflating demand they will bring inflation permanently under control and thereby induce an automatic recovery in output and employment.

(b) previous policies will deepen the depression, erode the industrial base of our economy and threaten its social and political stability.

(c) there are alternative policies; and

(d) the time has come to reject monetarist policies and consider urgently which alternative offers the best hope of sustained economic recovery.'

However, this was not a view shared by the leading industrialists

---

[1] S. Brittan, *Is There an Economic Consensus?*, London: Macmillan, 1973.

of the time who were urging the Government not to be deflected from its broad strategy against inflation by the rising volume of partisan opposition. Nor did they have the support of the City economists. As Tim Congdon remarked in 1983, 'The open question is not, are the 364 economists wrong, but how wrong are they?'

Most of the propositions in the survey are topical in that they reflect the theoretical and practical concerns of the last 20 years and, indeed, many of the questions that disturbed the 364 economists; many are of relevance to the formation of economic policy in the years that lie ahead. The survey reveals the extent to which certain fundamental presuppositions and opinions still govern the economic thinking of those people who will continue to shape and influence economic thought and policy into the next century.

The constitution of the Institute requires that all Trustees, Directors and Advisors dissociate themselves from the analysis and conclusions of its authors but they commend the comprehensive and timely survey undertaken by Professor Ricketts and Mr Shoesmith. The Institute of Economic Affairs has, for the past three decades, been instrumental in encouraging a wide-ranging debate on fundamental economic principles, and this *Research Monograph* should be read by everyone who is concerned with the teaching of the subject in schools, colleges of higher education, polytechnics and universities.

*May 1990*                                                    WALTER ALLAN

# Preface

As the author of one of the first attempts to consider the extent of agreement among economists,[1] I found the survey by Ricketts and Shoesmith made fascinating reading.

The new survey covers many more economists: 981 compared with 117 in my own case. The response rate was, however, remarkably similar and well within the range (35-45 per cent) normal in the more successful or luckier inquiries of this kind. The present investigation is thus clearly more ambitious in scope.

It does not, however, contain the control survey of the views of MPs and commentators which I attempted for the less technical questions. There is no reason, however, why the present authors, or others using their data, should not make the attempt in a subsequent study. One of the few ways to revive confidence in the wisdom of economists is to compare their responses to those of non-economists. I wonder, for instance, if a large majority of MPs of all parties are still opposed to differential peak-hour pricing for public transport, as they were in 1973.

A further difference is that many questions in my survey were derived from questions originally intended for students and were supposed to have correct answers. Ricketts and Shoesmith have a larger list, consisting of UK adaptations and developments of questions used in a series of international studies and devised specifically for the polling of economists. Perhaps for this reason my focus was on the extent of agreement whereas the present authors focus as much on disagreement. In both cases the core of the study is the Table listing the responses (Figure 9, between pp. 44 and 45) which the reader would be well advised to keep by his side.

But having duly noted the differences, among which the most important is the passage of time, I am impressed by the similarity of result. Looking at the answers deemed to be 'correct', I located a set of responses which I called the 'liberal economic orthodoxy'. This embodied a belief in competitive markets and pricing, but also in

---

[1] S. Brittan, *Is There an Economic Consensus?*, London: Macmillan, 1973.

redistribution of income, preferably by cash transfer. Environmental overspill was to be tackled by appropriate pricing devices. The outlook was also pretty Keynesian in the English post-war sense of believing that demand management affected output and employment and that fiscal policy was effective. This outlook was held, with whatever reservations, by about 75 per cent of the economists polled.

Looking at the Ricketts-Shoesmith results, the pattern seems remarkably similar. There is a fairly strong consensus, for instance, that agricultural price supports produce surpluses, and that deficiency payments are more efficient, that rent ceilings reduce the supply of rentable housing, and even that a minimum wage increases unemployment among young and unskilled workers.

Despite these mainstream answers, today's respondents—like their predecessors in the early 1970s—take every opportunity of showing how far removed they are from any 'minimum state' approach. The overwhelming majority favour state redistribution of income and a large majority endorse the slogan of 'more equality'. Indeed, the present authors conclude, from a run of recent international studies, what I could only suspect: namely, that British economists are more redistributive than those of any other country and also more Keynesian in the sense of accepting at least a short-run trade-off between unemployment and inflation. There is not only a very strong rejection of anything like a money supply rule, but there is not even a clear acceptance that inflation is primarily a monetary phenomenon.

In both the earlier survey and the present one, there was a rogue question which shattered the apparent consensus in favour of competitive price mechanism policies. In the earlier case, it was a question suggesting that subsidised public housing was less 'efficient' than direct social security payments. In the present case it is a suggestion that trade in human organs would be economically efficient. What the two very disparate questions have in common is the use of the question-begging word 'efficiency' in a contentious area. It is reassuring to find that simple predictive questions generate more consensus.

One apparent discrepancy between the two studies vanishes on closer examination. The present authors find no greater disagreement on macro-economic than on micro-economic questions. Nor did I. My evidence of deep-seated disagreements on the macro side was taken from outside my survey.[1] For the examiners' questions used in my survey served to bury rather than reveal 'vital areas of

---

[1] *Is There an Economic Consensus?*, *op. cit.*, especially Ch. 12.

public dispute'. So do many of the present questions, which focus on short-term effects and ignore longer-term or wider consequences: for example, the supposed stimulative effects of higher government expenditure compared to tax cuts.

No one with prior knowledge of the Ricketts-Shoesmith survey would have been the least bit surprised by the famous protest of 364 economists in 1981 against the Thatcher Government's macro-economic policies. Another politically significant sign is the overwhelming rejection of the view that government expenditure should be reduced—the main argument being between those who disagree and those who disagree strongly. The respondents could say (tongue in cheek) that they are in full accord with the Government, whose forward plans have for some years involved a real increase in public expenditure, accompanied by the hope of reducing it *only as a proportion of GDP*. But few on either side will be deceived on the likely results among this sample of the motion 'This House has no confidence in Her Majesty's Government'.

This is not the place to adjudicate. But there is something a little too goody-goody in British economists' characteristic responses. In 1973, they were asked about reforms in Communist economies, which were in the air long before Gorbachev. The approved 'correct' response, given by a large majority of economists, was that a freely operating market system can perform efficiently under 'socialism'. Since then the citizens of Eastern Europe have made their own decisive comments. But some doubts should have occurred to economists even in the early 1970s if they had been a little more familiar with works on the economics of property rights or public choice.

Today's goody-goody responses are embodied in the rejection of privatisation without measures to increase competition. Of course it is better if the two go together. But might not ownership, too, matter on a more subtle analysis? Indeed, British economists have been so preoccupied with catching up on American ones in their statistical and mathematical techniques that they have been laggard in coming to terms both with the critique of post-war demand management and with wider developments in political economy.[1] There is little sign of these lags being made up.

Perhaps the time has come for a less strenuous insistence on economics as a science. Most of the traditional doctrines about

---

[1] Some of these are listed in S. Brittan, *Participation without Politics*, Part One, sections vi and vii, first published (Hobart Paper 62) as early as 1975 by the Institute of Economic Affairs (2nd edn. 1979).

international trade, opportunity costs, 'supply and demand',and so on, are not falsifiable propositions; nor are they political value-judgements. They are intellectual frameworks or ways of looking at the world. (The same may also be true in the natural sciences to a much greater degree than their more naïve emulators among the social scientists would suppose.)

Economic arguments will not, moreover, be won by appeals to authority or majority votes any more than by political acceptability. One only has to look at the professional credentials of those who pronounce on economic matters—in letters to the press, for instance—to see that economists are now in the minority. Pronouncements, quite often backed by empirical research, come nowadays from economic historians, sociologists, management consultants, industrial relations specialists, business school theorists, financial analysts and applied engineers, to name only a few. Academic economists should surely be the last to apply closed-shop techniques to their competitors who, when they are joined by the dissentionists among their own number, often dominate the debate.

Economists do not need to pose as ersatz physicists. Philosophers and literary critics know more about their subjects than lay outsiders, without their being in a position to supply authoritative answers. Economists—or at least those among them who ponder grand questions such as the wealth of nations or the alternations of boom and slump—might reconcile themselves to being placed into the category of custodians of certain ways of thinking, yet still command respect.

It should provide satisfaction to know that most conventional businessmen's economics is wrong. Exports are not superior to imports; investment is not superior to consumption; manufacturing is not superior to services; the current balance of payments is not a nation's profit-and-loss account; incentives to maximise work effort make no sense and the highest possible GNP is a ridiculous object of policy. The main appeal of economic reasoning is its iconoclasm, which should always keep time-serving and sycophancy at bay.

*April 1990*                                             SAMUEL BRITTAN

# The Authors

MARTIN RICKETTS is Bernard Sunley Professor of Economic Organisation at the University of Buckingham. He studied economics at the universities of Newcastle upon Tyne and York, and was a research economist at the Industrial Policy Group (1970-72) and the Institute of Social and Economic Research at York (1974-77).

Since joining the staff of the University of Buckingham in 1977 he has pursued his interests in public choice, public policy, and the new institutional economics. His publications include *The Economics of Energy* (with Michael Webb), (1980), and *The Economics of Business Enterprise* (1987). He has also published in scholarly journals on government regulation, housing, and other aspects of public policy. Professor Ricketts is a member of the IEA's Advisory Council.

EDWARD SHOESMITH is Dean of the School of Sciences and Senior Lecturer in Statistics at the University of Buckingham. Before moving to Buckingham in 1977, he worked as a statistician and researcher in the Social Services Departments of two London Boroughs, and in the Social Statistics Division of the Central Statistics Office. He was the co-author, with Alan Peacock and Geoffrey Millner, of a report for the Arts Council of Great Britain, *Inflation and the Performed Arts* (1983). He has a first degree in Natural Sciences from the University of Cambridge and a post-graduate degree in Economics and Statistics from the University of York.

# Acknowledgements

The authors would like to thank Paul and Claire Sturges of the University of Loughborough for their help in giving us access to their list of economists compiled for *Who's Who in British Economics*. Edward Elgar kindly gave us permission to use the list in advance of publication. Alan Peacock and Mark Blaug gave us valuable assistance and advice when we were formulating the propositions which appeared in the survey, and both read and commented on drafts of the final report. The authors are, of course, entirely responsible for any shortcomings that may remain. We would also like to thank staff of the Department of Economics at the University of Nottingham who took part in a pilot survey and provided valuable anonymous comments on an early version of the survey. Finally, Roberto Rivero and Tunde Aiyegbusi, both of the University of Buckingham, gave valuable assistance in the task of processing the data as it was received.

*April 1990*                                                       M.R.
                                                                   E.S.

# Summary of Main Survey Results

## (1) The Response

o  (i)  Of 2,762 questionnaires sent out at the end of May 1989, 981 had been returned completed by the end of December 1989, a response rate of 35.5%.

   (ii) 90% of respondents were male, 79% had a master's degree or a doctorate, and 73% were employed in education.

   (iii) A higher proportion of women respondents than men specialise in the areas of welfare, urban economics, and labour.

   (iv) The specialisation of the respondent varies with employment. Business economists gave monetary theory and institutions most frequently as their specialisation. Economists in education gave general economic theory. Those in government mentioned industrial organisation, closely followed by labour, agriculture and natural resources.

   (v)  Government economists are young relative to academic economists. Nearly 40% of respondents who work for government are in their twenties compared with 5% of academic respondents. Almost 50% of the academic sample comprised people in their forties.     *(Section 5)*

## (2) Comparisons with Other Studies

*Extent of disagreement*

o  Compared with earlier surveys, two propositions are notable in producing a different distribution of responses in our sample.

   (i)  British economists were relatively agreed upon the proposition that 'unemployment can be reduced in the short run by accepting an increase in the rate of inflation'. Overseas studies show this as causing a high level of disagreement.

   (ii) The proposition that 'wage-price controls should be used

15

to control inflation' produced disagreement in our sample, but a high level of consensus (against the proposition) in earlier studies of opinion in America and Germany.

*(Section 6 (C) (i))*

### (3) Weight of Opinion

o British economists accept the redistributive role of government, attribute great influence to price signals, and are selective in their support for various types of government intervention.

 (i) A higher proportion of British economists agrees with the redistributive role of government than is true of economists in any other country for which survey evidence is available.

 (ii) Opinion on the effect of a minimum wage is midway between that in Europe and America in terms of the percentage agreeing that it increases unemployment. On rent control, a larger proportion of German and American economists predict a resulting decline in the supply of housing.

 (iii) British economists see consumer protection laws as relatively benign. They are strongly opposed to trade restrictions but less so than German, US and Canadian economists. *(Section 6 (C) (ii))*

### (4) Normative/Positive Comparisons

o Economists reach a higher level of agreement on purely predictive and factual statements than on normative and policy-related statements. The survey evidence does not suggest that there is greater agreement on micro-economic than on macro-economic propositions. *(Section 6 (D) and (E))*

### (5) Influence of Employment

o Opinion varied by the employment of respondents.

 (i) Business economists were more likely to disagree that government expenditure was more expansionary than tax cuts, to oppose the use of wage-price controls, to support a money supply rather than an interest-rate target, to agree with a zero inflation objective, and to oppose a more equal distribution of income.

 (ii) Government economists were more likely to agree that a minimum wage increases unemployment and that the replacement of domestic local rates by the Community Charge ('poll tax') will increase the price of housing.

*(Section 7 (i))*

## (6) Influence of Age and Sex

o Opinion varied by the age and sex of the respondent.

   (i) Young economists were less convinced of some of the micro-economic propositions than their elders. Young people were less likely to agree (or agree so strongly) that a minimum wage increased unemployment or that rent control reduced the supply of housing. They attributed less influence on trade flows to non-tariff barriers, were less concerned about the power of the unions, and much more favourable to a more egalitarian distribution of income.

   (ii) Female economists were distinctly less 'monetarist' in their approach to policy. They were more inclined to doubt that inflation is a monetary phenomenon, to oppose a money growth rule, and to favour the redistributive role of government. Female economists were more inclined to believe that financial markets suffer from 'short-termism', and inclined to disagree that trade in human organs would be efficient. *(Section 7 (ii) and (iii))*

## (7) Influence of Specialistion

o (i) Formal qualifications have very limited impact on the responses to the propositions. The main effect is to distinguish those who have a degree in economics from those who do not.

   (ii) The specialisation of the respondent was related to attitudes to some technical propositions concerning methods of agricultural support and the importance of non-tariff barriers to trade, where specialists were notably more likely to agree with the propositions than were other respondents. Agricultural economists regarded deficiency payments as more efficient than price support schemes, and international economists regarded non-tariff barriers as having a greater effect on trade flows than tariff barriers. Specialists in monetary economics, however, were less inclined than other economists to agree with the proposition that the European Monetary System was superior to a régime of floating exchange rates.

(iii) The possibility that opinion might influence specialisation as well as the other way round was suggested by the association between support for income redistribution and specialisation in labour economics, welfare programmes, consumer economics, or urban economics.

*(Section 8)*

## (8) Friedman's and Samuelson's Conjectures

o (i) Evidence is presented indicating that opinions about policy are systematically related to relevant empirical propositions (Friedman's conjecture).

(ii) Evidence is presented consistent with the view that, for given opinions about empirical matters, differing distributional judgements influence opinion about policy (Samuelson's conjecture). *(Section 9)*

## (9) Economic Doctrine

o Evidence was sought for the existence of groups of propositions to which responses were related. A group of such propositions was found to contain correlated attitudes to income redistribution, wage-price control, government spending, inflation as a monetary phenomenon, a money supply target, consumer protection laws, and control of take-overs and financial markets. A further group of correlated propositions centred on micro-economics and the efficiency of markets. Our results are similar to those found in earlier work (Kearl *et al.*, 1979). *(Section 10)*

# ONE

# Introduction

Economists often do not agree with one another. With this proposition at least there would, we suspect, be little disagreement. The differing predictions of macro-economic models compete for the attention of headline writers, the conflicting views of advisors can compromise the political stability of governments, and the feuds of academic theorists seem, on occasions, not far removed from the pages of that popular literary genre—the campus novel.

For a short time in the 1950s the seductive idea became popular that economics could be viewed as a science, similar in methodology to the 'natural' sciences. Keynesian economics was at the height of its influence (in the United Kingdom at least), and there were the associated developments in National Income Accounting and statistical modelling which contributed to the image of a true science in the making. Although Keynes himself explicitly rejected the view that economics should be treated as a 'pseudo-natural science', his naïve belief that much of the subject could be made relatively non-controversial implied a level of consensus which has not in practice been approached. On monetary matters, for example, Keynes believed it possible that statements could be made which were as uncontroversial as the statements of scientists on the principles of electricity.

The claim of economics to be able to control the level of employment and the value of money, and thus to secure the population against both mass unemployment and inflation, was an impressive one. However, as time and events gradually eroded this foundation upon which the regard of most people rested, the status of economics as the most developed of the social sciences was increasingly called into question. Instead of the respect and awe popularly attributed to the high priesthood of the true sciences, economists became the butt of popular jokes (frequently set on desert islands) and usually involving the tendency of members of the profession to change their minds, or their ability to hold entirely contradictory opinions, or to imagine totally unrealistic conditions. Scientific credibility, like that of cabinet government, has something to do, as Lord Melbourne remarked, not with what people are saying, but with their capacity to say the same thing. This central requirement seems to have defeated economists in the half-century since the Second World War.

Although this description of the general process of loss in public esteem is one which many practitioners of economics will recognise, it is pertinent to consider in more detail the nature of disagreement between economists. Public perceptions may be wrong or over-simplified, and it may be of some importance to discover *why* economists disagree, whether they disagree with equal vehemence about all economic questions or whether there are still areas of broad consensus. It is widely thought, for example, that disputes are more prevalent on macro-economic issues than on micro-economic ones. Schultze (1985) writes that

> 'The vast majority of our profession share a common view on most micro-economic policy issues. But we are widely split over macro-economic theory and policy'. (p. 1)

## Sources of Disagreement

Disagreement in economics can derive from several sources.

### (i) Formal Logic

Arguments about the properties of purely abstract economic models are not unknown, but such arguments may in principle be resolved by the careful definition of terms and the checking of deductive methods. The continuing attempts of economists to clarify terms and refine abstract models have, perhaps paradoxically, contributed to the view that economics is not relevant to the real world. Yet without these models it is difficult to see how any claim to scientific status could be defended. Indeed, for a philosopher like Hobbes, it was precisely this attention to the close definition of terms and the correct process of logical reasoning that was the defining characteristic of science.

### (ii) Empirical Evidence

The 20th century has seen the development of a rather different perspective on science. For many writers science has come to be associated not merely with the consistent application of logical reasoning to an initial set of axioms, but with the ability to make predictions about observable phenomena which are then capable of being refuted. This view is associated with Karl Popper and, in the particular context of economics, with a celebrated essay by Milton Friedman (1953). This *Research Monograph* is not the place to become embroiled in the many subtle points of difference between writers in this field. It is widely, and we assume correctly asserted, however, that most economists officially embrace ideas which are at least loosely associated with the 'falsificationist' position. McCloskey (1983) outlines 11 precepts which economists are supposed to support (in principle, at any rate, although not necessarily in practice), such as 'only the observable implications (or predictions) of a theory matter to its truth' (p. 484).

## Battleground of empirical testing

In the present context the importance of these debates lies in the implication that the ability of economic theory to withstand empirical testing becomes the means of judging success or failure. Unfortunately, the result seems to have been not the development of a set of well-established tried-and-tested propositions around which the profession could muster, but an additional battleground upon which to fight. It is rather as if the litmus test resulted not in a clear and agreed 'red' or 'blue' result, either confirming or denying stated predictions, but in a consistently replicated murky purple colour defying any agreed classification but sufficiently close to both predictions to encourage each side. Onlookers must frequently feel like Alice as she watched the battle between the white and red knights in *Through the Looking Glass:*

'"It was a glorious victory wasn't it?" said the white knight as he came panting up. "I don't know," Alice said doubtfully.'

Disagreement therefore may frequently derive from different ideas about what constitutes a suitable test of a theory when, as is always the case in the social sciences, it is impossible artificially to construct controlled experiments.

Part of the problem of empirical testing involves our natural proclivity to observe whatever we believe is necessary to confirm our preconceived ideas. The physicists who first 'confirmed' Einstein's prediction that light is subject to the gravitational attraction of massive bodies (through a set of observations during an eclipse of the sun in West Africa in 1919) have subsequently been shown to have misinterpreted their photographic evidence. The scientists who were hoaxed by the 'discovery' of Piltdown Man were too anxious to accept evidence which so perfectly suited their theoretical view. If people in areas of such hard science are prone to these mistakes, the temptations facing researchers in the social sciences, where the desire to 'prove' various propositions might be even more personally compelling, must be even greater.

## (iii) Vested Interests

Economics challenges not merely the powers of reason and the ability to conduct empirical tests (the first two sources of possible disagreement) but it can also present a challenge to vested interests. This third source of conflict has been recognised for centuries as of great importance. When economists discuss matters of public policy they cannot avoid making judgements about what constitutes the public good, and although they may search for ways of compensating any losers, their recommendations will in practice offend many people. Hobbes well expressed the point in *Leviathan*. Men, he argued,

> 'appeale from custome to reason, and from reason to custome, as it serves their turn; receding from custome when their interest requires it, and setting themselves against reason, as oft as reason is against them: Which is the cause, that the doctrine of right and wrong, is perpetually disputed, both by the pen and the sword: whereas the doctrine of lines, and figures is not so; because men care not, in that subject what be truth, as a thing that crosses no mans ambition, profit, or lust'. (p. 166)

That powerful vested interests may attempt to cast doubt on economic analysis when its conclusions seem uncongenial is compatible with a great deal of disagreement and discussion, but it does not in itself imply that economists will disagree among themselves. The latter conclusion would follow only if economists were primarily 'hired guns' (a metaphor coined by Alan Peacock) whose interests coincided with those of the interest groups which they represented. We would then expect, in a Hobbesian world, to see business economists supporting the claims of monopolists, others attacking established monopoly positions, academic economists in public sector universities arguing for the expansion of public expenditure in higher education, and so forth.

An alternative possibility is that, although economists will naturally have their own interests to consider, these, in any individual case, will influence judgement in only a limited number of areas, leaving an economist's pronouncements over a large range of policy matters relatively untainted. Indeed, the possibility has even been mooted that the reputation of an economist is a valuable asset which may, to a sufficient degree, depend upon avoiding too close an association with particular interest groups.

## (iv) Ethical Judgements

Even where the pronouncements of economists can plausibly be considered disinterested, disagreements about policy questions might still be expected. Disagreement can arise from sources other than divergences in personal interests or differing interpretations of empirical evidence. Ethical considerations will also be important. A clear distinction, it is argued, can be drawn between statements which depend upon implicit ethical judgements (for example, 'the government ought to introduce a minimum wage') and purely scientific statements which depend on making predictions about the consequences of different courses of action (for example, 'A minimum wage will leave the rate of unemployment unchanged'). The latter statement is, at least in principle, refutable and does not depend on opinions concerning what ought to be done.

This distinction between 'positive' (scientific) statements and 'normative' statements involving value-judgements is at the centre of modern disputes over methodology in economics. The proposition that these two classes of statement are quite separate in the sense that 'one cannot deduce ought from is' has become known as 'Hume's guillotine' after David Hume's statement of the principle in his *Treatise of Human Nature*. Although Hume's guillotine is a principle well known to economists, the is-ought distinction is not uncontroversial among philosophers. A review of the disputes which have surrounded the is-ought distinction, and the attacks which have been made on the very possibilty of a value-free social science, can be found in Blaug (1980). Whatever the purely philosophical difficulties associated with Hume's guillotine, economists frequently refer to the is-ought distinction when discussing the nature of disagreements in the discipline, and in later sections of this report we have attempted to separate the propositions of the survey into different classes.

Milton Friedman's view (at least as expressed in his 1953 essay) is that

'differences about economic policy ... derive predominantly from different predictions ... rather than from fundamental differences in basic values' (p. 25).

and this has gained wide acceptance by members of the profession anxious to establish their role as producers of disinterested technical advice. As Friedman recognised, however, his judgement concerning the source of differing opinions about public policy 'is itself a "positive" statement to be accepted or rejected on the basis of empirical evidence' (p. 25). Is it true, for example, that people who agree about predictions also tend to agree about policy? Is it true that the general level of agreement in the profession concerning empirical matters varies positively with the level of agreement on related policy questions? An alternative view might be that disagreement about policy issues does not in general derive mainly from disagreement about 'positive' predictions. Thurow (1986), for example, argues that

'Different economists have different answers to the "ought" question, even if they agree on the technical outcome and the distribution of gains and losses'. (p. 25)

Similarly, Samuelson (1959) speculates that differences in economic opinion exist because most decisions 'involve ethical ends that transcend positive science' (p. 192). Note that both these statements contradict the optimism of Friedman, and imply that agreement about predictions is no guarantee of agreement about policy.

In economics it is by no means straightforward to separate, as Hobbes expressed it, the doctrine of right and wrong from the doctrine of lines and figures. Even a cursory perusal of a modern economics textbook will reveal sufficient lines and figures to satisfy the appetite of all but the most ardent geometer. Yet it is not clear whether this formal geometry, which plays such a large part in the education of the average economist, has succeeded in ridding the profession of unnecessary disputes. Propositions which 'cross no man's ambition, profit, or lust' may on occasion form the subject of academic seminars, but they hardly make up the stuff of public controversy. Economic disputes are interesting very largely *because* they involve an amalgam of vested interests, ethical judgements, and empirical assertions which are usually almost impossible to test. In this *Research Monograph* we attempt, nevertheless, to use survey evidence to disentangle some of these forces, and to look for the sources of disagreement between economists.

# TWO

# Evidence From Earlier Surveys

## Brittan's Pioneering Survey

One of the first attempts to consider the extent of agreement between economists, and to compare the attitudes of economists with those of journalists and politicians, was that of Samuel Brittan (1973). Brittan sent to a sample of economists and others a set of multiple choice questions selected from various versions of a Test of Economics Comprehension prepared by the Esmée Fairbairn Research Centre at Heriot-Watt University. Usable replies were received from 117 economists and 91 Members of Parliament. Questions covered such topics as the pricing of bus and underground fares in the rush hour, the efficiency of cash versus 'in kind' benefits, the allocative role of prices generally, the causes of unemployment in a market economy, and so forth. The objective was not to test the extent to which 'correct' answers were given to the questions, but to investigate the degree of consensus and the extent to which economists took a systematically different view from politicians and commentators.

Brittan found, for example, that 88% of economists supported the charging of higher fares in peak periods, whereas 80% of Labour MPs and 60% of Conservative MPs were opposed. On micro-economic issues 'economists achieved a substantial degree of consensus, which set them apart from both Labour and Conservative politicians' (p. 78). On macro-economic questions involving unemployment, growth, inflation and international monetary stability, on the other hand, Brittan discerned a 'dissenting minority (of economists) of some intellectual respectability' (p. 78). There is some evidence in Brittan's survey, therefore, that economists are more inclined to agree about micro-economic than about macro-economic questions.

When processing the replies to the questionnaire. Brittan undertook the enormous task of looking carefully at each response and reading any accompanying explanations and elaborations written by respondents. This allowed him to interpret replies and to become acquainted with objections to and interpretations of the various questions.

'I shudder to think . . . what this enquiry would have yielded if it had been undertaken by the fashionable computerised methods, in which only rigidly pre-specified alternatives would have been digested by a literal-minded magnetic tape . . .' (p. 25).

More recent work, including the survey reported in this *Research Monograph*, pays little heed to Brittan's intuition and proceeds largely on the basis which he criticises. This is not to say that marginal comments were ignored in our own survey, but simply that there was no systematic attempt to embody them within the statistical analysis. Comments and letters accompanying the replies do, of course, inform the commentary surrounding the statistical results in later sections.

### Kearl's Survey of US Economists

A survey by Kearl *et al.* (1979) provides the starting point for the series of studies of which the present work can be seen as a continuation. Kearl sent a questionnaire to a stratified random sample of 600 members of the American Economic Association (300 academics, 150 employed in the private non-academic sector, and 150 economists in government appointments). The questionnaire contained 30 short statements such as 'Wage-price controls should be used to control inflation', and respondents were asked to record their attitudes using the categories 'generally agree', 'agree with provisions', or 'generally disagree'. Just over one-third of the questionnaires were completed and returned. The degree of consensus on each question was calculated using a 'relative entropy' measure, the properties of which we will discuss in detail in Section 6(A) (below, p. 41). Kearl found that the survey responses were consistent with the hypotheses that there was greater consensus on micro-economic than on macro-economic issues, and on propositions involving the word 'can' compared with those involving the word 'should'.

### Frey's Survey of Four European Countries

True to the traditions of the subject, however, Kearl's survey has been followed by others which complicate the results. Economists in different countries, it appears, disagree about the issues most likely to result in disagreement. Frey *et al.* (1984) sent a questionnaire containing 27 of Kearl's propositions to a sample of economists in Austria, France, Germany, and Switzerland, thus supplementing the data produced by the initial survey. An analysis of the combined responses of 936 economists did not confirm that micro and positive propositions produced less disagreement than macro and normative propositions.

'The result for the United States does not apply to our international study, neither does it apply to any of the European countries on its own.' (p. 990)

Frey's study also found evidence of pronounced differences in the response patterns of economists between countries. In particular, American, German and Swiss economists took a systematically different view from their French and Austrian colleagues concerning the role of the price mechanism and the appropriate scope of government intervention.

'Overall, the discussion suggests that the American, German and Swiss economists are clearly more in support of the price system, competition and therewith neo-classical economics, and that the Austrian and French economists are less convinced of the price system and therefore have a higher tendency to agree with interventions of the government into the economy.' (p. 993)

## Block and Walker on Canada

Block and Walker (1988) provide the most recent replication of Kearl's experiment using the same 27 propositions as Frey *et al.*, but sampling Canadian opinion. As expected, Canadian economists had more in common with those in the United States than with those in Europe. However, Block and Walker could not establish that greater consensus existed over positive and micro-economic questions than over normative and macro-economic ones. In this respect their results are similar to those of Frey *et al.* for European economists. In addition, they provide interesting information on how responses to the propositions differed according to the age, sex and education of the respondent. Whereas, for example, 72% of males generally agreed with the proposition that tariffs and quotas reduce economic welfare, only 39% of females chose this response category. Comparisons with the results of our survey are provided in a later section.

# THREE

# Objectives of the IEA Study

No attitude survey similar to those discussed in Section 2 had been undertaken in the UK by the beginning of 1989, and the primary purpose of the survey reported in this *Research Monograph* was to discover whether the state of professional opinion in Britain differed in significant respects from that found in other countries. Our interests were not entirely confined to international comparisons and the replication of earlier work, however, and we attempted to modify and extend the inquiry in various ways. A list of broad objectives is as follows:

o To generate and collate the responses of a sample of economists in the UK to various economic propositions.

o To measure by calculating relative entropy scores, or by other means, the level of disagreement or dispersion associated with each proposition.

o To rank the propositions by level of consensus and compare the ranking with results generated by similar surveys in other countries.

o To test for significant relationships between the responses and demographic factors such as age, sex, employment, specialisation and formal education.

o To compare responses to micro-economic propositions with those to macro-economic propositions, and to compare responses to normative and non-normative propositions.

o To investigate whether systematic relationships exist between responses to the propositions contained in the survey.

# FOUR

# The Questionnaire

The questionnaire is reproduced in Appendix 1. It consists of 35 propositions, 20 of which are identical to, or slight modifications of, propositions appearing in earlier surveys. These 20 propositions are marked with an asterisk (which did not appear on the questionnaire sent to the sample of economists). Compared with the original survey of US economists by Kearl, the differences between versions of the common 20 propositions mainly concern substitution of words such as 'central bank' for 'Federal Reserve', or 'developed industrial nations' for 'the United States'.

Proposition 3 was rephrased to allow for the passage of time so that reference to oil price rises in 'the past three years' in Kearl's survey became 'the past five years' in Frey *et al.*, and 'the 1970s' in both Block's survey and ours. Another possibly significant change in phraseology occurs in proposition 13. The version used in earlier surveys states that 'In the short run, unemployment can be reduced by increasing the rate of inflation' whereas we used the phrase 'by accepting an increase in the rate of inflation'. Presumably the question as used by Kearl was designed to elicit opinions about the slope of the 'short-run Phillips Curve'[1] and by implication the extent to which the 'rational expectations'[2] debate had influenced assessments of the freedom of manoeuvre available to government in the conduct of macro-economic policy. Our own version, by using the word 'accept', merely attempted to make clear that the existence of a technical trade-off outside the control of government was being postulated.

Of the propositions which are comparable with those in earlier surveys the greatest rephrasing is found in proposition 26 on the trade unions. 'The economic power of labor unions should be significantly curtailed' became in our survey 'The power of the trade

---

[1] Conventionally the Phillips curve relates the rate of inflation to the level of unemployment. Initially, unanticipated increases in the rate of inflation were associated with declining unemployment.

[2] More sophisticated models of expectations formation have questioned the extent of the trade-off until, in the extreme case of 'rational expectations' with perfect information, it is argued that the trade-off disappears altogether.

unions is not a significant economic problem'. We would expect a strong inverse correlation between responses to these two versions of the proposition, and felt that the latter version was more appropriate following a decade of reforms to the labour market in the UK. It could be argued that the two versions are so different that they cannot be used in comparisons between survey results. However, we proceeded on the basis that comparisons would be made both including and excluding the proposition on trade unions, and, as will be seen in later sections, our results were not influenced significantly either way.

## New propositions

After removing those propositions from Kearl's survey which appeared either too dated or too specific to American conditions and preoccupations, our total of 35 propositions made room for 15 'new entries'. Numbers 4 to 9 inclusive involve topical micro-economic issues including privatisation, regulation, take-overs, the 'community charge', and the incidence of divorce. This last proposition was included because it involved an area widely considered beyond the realm of purely economic analysis, and it was of interest to see how far economists were prepared to stretch the use of theory, and whether correlations existed between responses to this and other more conventional propositions.

Propositions 14 to 16 add to the section on macro-economics and refer to issues of relevance to the 1980s—the importance of non-tariff barriers, the macro-economic effects of tax reductions, and the relative impact of debt finance compared with tax finance of the public sector. Propositions 21 to 25 concern the efficiency of certain markets or the role of public policy in controlling them. Apart from number 24 they are new entries to the survey. Proposition 22 concerning a market in human organs for transplant purposes is another attempt to investigate how 'robust' are economists' views on the social functions of markets. Finally, proposition 32 on the European Monetary System replaces Kearl's question on floating exchange rates, but was too distant a substitute to permit direct comparison between the surveys; while proposition 33 is a straightforward attempt to obtain information about support for a particular policy objective (the elimination of inflation).

## Order of propositions, and response categories

Apart from the number of propositions involved, our survey differed from earlier ones in the *order* in which the common propositions appeared. The first 16 items consist of predictive statements, some phrased as theoretical and conditional hypotheses (such as number 6 on divorce) and others requiring knowledge of the facts of a given situation (for instance, number 14 on tariff and non-tariff barriers). From proposition 17 onwards words such as 'superior', 'should', 'better', 'more important', 'economic welfare', and 'economic efficiency' make their appearance. This particular structure was not used in earlier surveys where micro- and macro-economic statements and normative and positive statements were presented with no apparent regard for order.

Perhaps the major departure from earlier surveys involved our decision to increase the number of response categories from three to five. In doing so we faced the obvious danger that comparisons with earlier work would be compromised. On the other hand, the restricted nature of the responses available on the earlier surveys had been subject to criticism, and the established categories appeared rather 'asymmetrical'—permitting two types of agreement but only one category of disagreement. Our five categories gave respondents more options, including the option of 'sitting on the fence', and were presented symmetrically, although it is debatable whether 'agree with reservations' represents precisely the state of mind with respect to 'agreement' that 'generally disagree' represents with respect to 'disagreement'.

# FIVE

# The Response

Altogether 2,762 questionnaires were sent out using a mailing list compiled by Paul and Clair Sturges at the University of Loughborough for *Who's Who in Economics*; 981 replies had been received by 1 January 1990 (about seven months after the mailing), a response rate of 35·5%. This response rate is virtually the same as that obtained by Kearl (35%) and by Block (35·9%), but less than the 45·2% return rate of Frey *et al*. It is worth noting that the surveys conducted overseas were all based on the membership lists of professional associations, for example, the American Economic Association, the Canadian Economics Association, the Association Nationale des Docteurs en Science Economiques, and so forth. The list compiled at the University of Loughborough contained members of several different organisations, was not limited to a single dominant association, and had involved extensive inquiries amongst university and polytechnic departments. It is not unlikely that the differences between countries thrown up by surveys of this sort are to some extent explained by the differing meaning which is attached to the label 'economist' and the consequent differences which exist in the structure of the profession.

Table 1 indicates the breakdown of the respondents using the personal information requested in the first part of the questionnaire.

As expected, the vast majority of the respondents were employed in education and were male (see also Figures 1 and 3). Kearl *et al*. stratified their sample with one-quarter of the questionnaires going to people known to be employed in private business and one-quarter to economists employed in government agencies. As a result, similar response rates across the strata ensured that over one-quarter of respondents were employed in business. In our case only about 8% were in this category (Table 1 and Figure 3), although our larger sample size gave a greater absolute number of respondents than in Kearl's survey. Block's survey was not stratified by employment category and the proportion of respondents in education was over 75%—an even higher percentage than ours. Compared with our survey, Block's

**Table 1:**
**Characteristics of the Sample**

| | % | | % |
|---|---|---|---|
| **(i) Employment:** | | **(iv) Age:** | |
| Education | 73 | Twenties | 11 |
| Business | 8 | Thirties | 29 |
| Government | 17 | Forties | 40 |
| Other | 2 | Fifties | 16 |
| No Reply | 0 | Sixties | 3 |
| | | Seventies | 1 |
| | | No Reply | < 1 |
| **(ii) Sex:** | | | |
| Male | 90 | **(v) Specialisation:** | |
| Female | 10 | Gen. Theory | 17 |
| No Reply | < 1 | Ind. org., Tec. | 13 |
| | | Welfare-Con. | 9 |
| | | Labour-Popn. | 8 |
| | | Mon. th. + Inst. | 8 |
| **(iii) Qualifications:** | | Agric. + Nat. res. | 8 |
| Doctorates | 37 | Quantitative | 8 |
| Master's Degree | 42 | Internat. Econ. | 7 |
| Bachelor's | 18 | Growth-Develop. | 7 |
| No Degree | 2 | Bus. fin., Acc. | 5 |
| No Reply | < 1 | No Reply | 9 |

*Note:* The figures are based on 981 respondents. They are rounded to the nearest whole per cent, and may therefore not sum to 100%. The relatively large proportion of non-responses to the 'Specialisation' item results from respondents failing to rank their areas of interest in the way they were invited to do.

was also more male-dominated, with only 5% of women respondents, and had a higher proportion of respondents under the age of thirty (19% in Block's survey compared with 11% in ours). The age distribution of our respondents is illustrated in Figure 2. Information on the area of specialisation of the respondent (the area ranked first in answer to question 6) reveals that 'general economics' is the most popular followed by 'industrial organisation', with the remaining respondents spread quite evenly over the other categories (Table 1, Figure 4).

Cross-tabulations show highly significant relationships between personal characteristics such as age and occupation, specialisation and occupation, sex and specialisation, etc. For example, the government was the main employer (56%) of respondents in their twenties. Further, a higher proportion (38%) of government economists were in this age category than in any other. In contrast, the modal age class for business economists was 30-39, and that for academics was 40-49. Approaching half (48%) of academic respondents were in this age range. Figure 6 summarises this information. As might be expected, women tended to be younger than men (Figure 5), tended to specialise in welfare and labour matters (Figure 7), and were over-represented in government employment.

Areas of specialisation differed by employment category (Figure 8). Business economists specialise in monetary policy, fiscal policy, and industrial matters (presumably reflecting employment by banks, stockbrokers, and consulting firms). Over 20% of specialists in monetary theory and policy were employed by business firms, although economists employed in business accounted for little more than 8% of the entire sample. The government employs economists disproportionately in the areas of natural resources and labour, according to the responses to the survey; 30% of specialists in agriculture and natural resources were employed by government compared with about 1% (a single respondent) employed by business.

## Figure 1:
## Distribution of the sample by sex

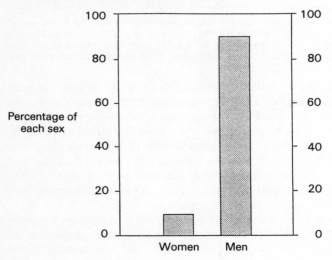

The percentages are based on those who responded to the relevant item on the questionnaire.

## Figure 2:
## Distribution of the sample by age-group

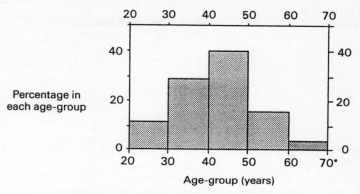

Percentage in each age-group

Age-group (years)

The percentages are based on those who responded
to the relevant item on the questionnaire.

*The very small number of respondents aged 70+ have been included in this final
age-group.

## Figure 3:
## Distribution of the sample by type of employment

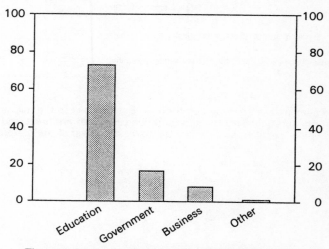

The percentages are based on those who responded
to the relevant item on the questionnaire.

**Figure 4:**
**Distribution of the sample by area of specialisation**

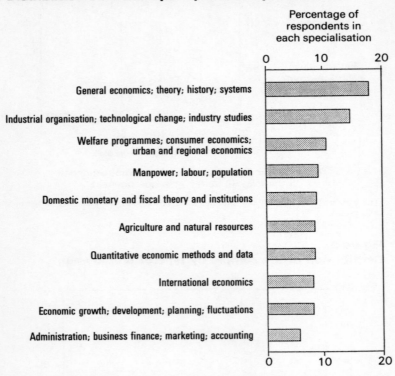

The percentages are based on those who responded to the relevant item on the questionnaire. The specialisation categories are presented from most popular choice at the top to least popular at the bottom.

**Figure 5:**
**Age distribution of the sample by sex**

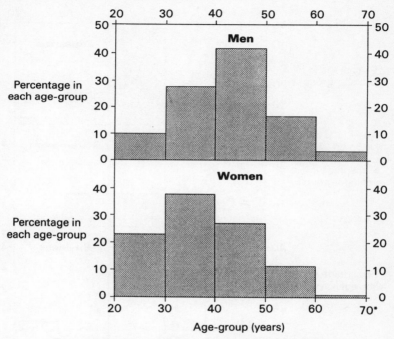

The percentages are based on those who responded to
both the relevant items on the questionnaire.

*The very small number of respondents aged 70+ have been included in this final
age-group.

**Figure 6:**
**Age distribution of the sample by type of employment**

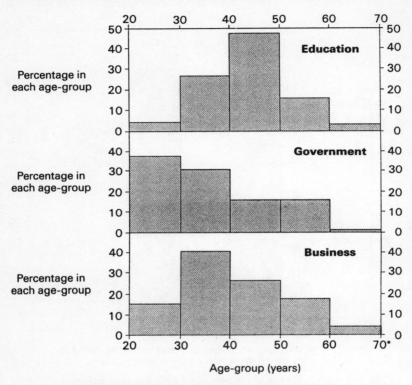

The percentages are based on those who responded to
both the relevant items on the questionnaire.

*The very small number of respondents aged 70+ have been included in this final
age-group.

**Figure 7:**
**Distribution of the sample by area of specialisation,
classified by sex**

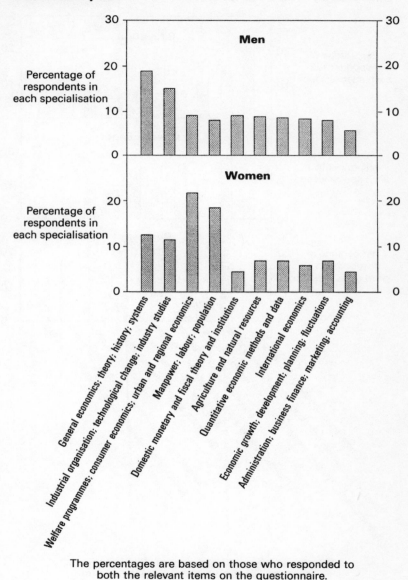

The percentages are based on those who responded to
both the relevant items on the questionnaire.

## Figure 8:
## Distribution of the sample by area of specialisation, classified by type of employment

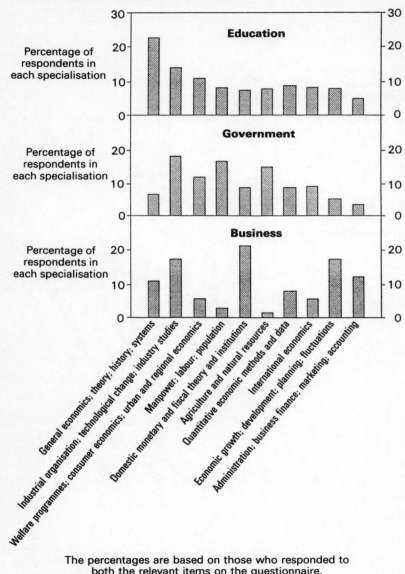

The percentages are based on those who responded to
both the relevant items on the questionnaire.

# SIX

# What Do Economists Disagree About?

## A. Measures of Disagreement

There are several different ways in which we commonly interpret the phrase 'amount of disagreement'. There is, first, the idea that if opinion can be defined by a single variable (for example, the desired amount of spending on the Health Service), disagreement between any two people could be represented by the 'distance' between them. There is less disagreement between two people wanting spending of respectively £100 and £200 per head than between two people wanting spending of respectively zero and £400 per head. In a population of many people the greatest combined 'distance' between all pairs of individuals would occur if half the population took one 'extreme' view and half the population took the other. Maximum disagreement would be reflected in a balanced but 'polarised' set of opinions.

The other common interpretation of disagreement in a group of people is that the wider the spread or variety of opinions held, the greater the level of disagreement exhibited. In the example of the previous paragraph, maximum disagreement measured by 'total distance' existed even though only two different opinions were to be found in the population. If, instead of concentration around certain extremes, the population included every possible shade of opinion evenly spread across the entire feasible range, it would be possible to argue that this represented a greater amount of disagreement even than the case of polarisation. This might be particularly so if opinion on an issue could not plausibly be quantified and measured cardinally along a single dimension.

### 'Relative entropy'—the measure of disagreement

In this survey we have used 'relative entropy' as a measure of disagreement. In doing so we have followed the precedent set in the other studies mentioned in Section 2 and have thereby implicitly adopted a definition of disagreement based on variety of opinion. The calculation of relative entropy is explained in Appendix 2 (below,

p. 92). Entropy and therefore disagreement according to this measure are at their greatest if equal proportions of the population hold every possible opinion. Given the five response categories included in our questionnaire, this simply means that if 20% of respondents fall into each category, maximum entropy is achieved and the relative entropy measure takes the value of 1 (or 100%). Minimum entropy (i.e. a value of zero) occurs if the entire sample of responses falls into a single category.

Because some of our results are presented in terms of this measure of disagreement it is important to recognise that interpretation requires care. In particular, the following points are pertinent.

o A low entropy figure (high level of agreement) cannot be interpreted as implying strength of professional opinion either in favour of or against a particular proposition. For example, perfect agreement would be registered if the entire sample ticked the 'neither agree nor disagree' box in response to a given proposition. Economists would be united, but only in their unwillingness to express an opinion either way. If a relative entropy figure of zero were obtained from the responses to the proposition on the European Monetary System, for example, this might simply reveal that no economist had yet made up his or her mind on the issue.

o Use of the entropy concept requires us to suppress some of our instinctive ideas about disagreement and 'distance' between opinions. For example, from one point of view, if half of all respondents ticked 'strongly agree' and the other half ticked 'strongly disagree', this would represent maximum disagreement. We have already seen that this is not true of the entropy measure. From the point of view of entropy, there would be no distinction between this 'polarised' case and another case in which half the sample ticked 'strongly agree' and the other half ticked 'agree with reservations'. In short, from the perspective of an approach to disagreement based on 'distance', entropy fails to distinguish between a case representing maximum disagreement and another representing a situation close to perfect agreement.

o In international comparisons of professional opinion it would be a mistake to think of similar entropy values for a particular proposition as implying agreement between economists in different countries. Clearly a proposition which results in an entropy value of zero in both England and France is not necessarily one on which English and French economists agree. All that is implied is that the English agree with one another and the French agree with one another. This is quite compatible with the two sets of economists holding totally opposed views. Similarly, if we observe that the ranking of propositions by levels of relative entropy is similar in two countries, we cannot deduce that there is similarity of opinion across countries. We can conclude only that, at least according to this particular measure of disagreement, the propositions which result in the most disagreement in one country are the same as those which cause the most disagreement in the other.

## B. Initial Ranking of Survey Propositions

Figure 9 provides, in summary form, the distribution of responses to each proposition, the mean response score for each proposition, and the relative entropy value. The propositions are ordered by relative entropy, with those giving rise to the most dispersed opinion at the top (i.e. agreement increases as we move down the table). The mean response score was calculated by assigning values of plus 2 and minus 2 respectively to 'strongly agree' and 'strongly disagree', plus 1 and minus 1 to qualified agreement and disagreement, and zero to 'neither agree nor disagree'. The final mean score might be interpreted, therefore, as an overall measure of 'balance of opinion' one way or the other. As might be expected, marked disagreement (high relative entropy) tends to be associated with a mean response score close to zero (opinions tending to cancel each other out), and low entropy propositions are associated with higher absolute mean response scores. The relationship is not perfect, however, partly for the reasons discussed above (in subsection (A)).

Consider the proposition at the top of Figure 9. The little bar chart shows the distribution of responses to the statement 'Permitting trade in human organs for transplant purposes would be economically efficient'. It can be seen that opinion is spread fairly evenly over four of the five possible categories of response. Only a few respondents were in strong agreement, but the most chosen category was 'agree with reservations', and the other categories contained substantial numbers of respondents. This spread is sufficient to produce a high relative entropy value of 95%, and this is represented visually by the black portion of the 'clock face' on the far right of the figure. Moving down the table of propositions, the black portion of the associated clocks gets smaller and the white portion gets bigger, indicating that the 'degree of agreement' is increasing. What might loosely be termed 'the balance of opinion' is indicated on the gauge between the frequency diagram and the clock. For each proposition a shaded area extends outwards from the centre of the gauge. The further to the left this area extends the greater the general extent of agreement with the proposition. The further to the right, the stronger and/or more extensive the degree of disagreement with the proposition. In the case of the first proposition in Figure 9 it is seen that those who agree and those who disagree roughly counterbalance each other, and there is only a very small shaded area discernible on the side of disagreement.

The fourth and fifth propositions in Figure 9 are also high entropy propositions (92% and 91% respectively). It should be noted, however, that the distribution of responses in the frequency chart next to each proposition is quite different from that of the first on the list. For the propositions that 'inflation is primarily a monetary phenomenon' and 'the power of the trade unions is not a significant economic problem', opinion is rather symmetrical, with those in strong agreement counterbalancing those in strong disagreement, and those agreeing with reservations almost exactly matching those in general disagreement. Once again, therefore, the 'balance of opinion' is almost exactly at the centre of the gauge showing the mean response score.

That the entropy value is not the same as strength of opinion can be seen by considering proposition 34 (the eighth in the order of Figure 9). Proposition 34 asserts that 'the level of government spending should be reduced'. Comparing the distribution of responses with those for proposition 26 on the power of the trade unions, both differences and similarities can be observed. First, it is evident that the balance of opinion is hostile to proposition 34. The two most popular categories are D and E. Most economists disagree with the proposition that government spending should be reduced and this is reflected in the gauge which shows a mean response score of minus 0·7. On the other hand, there is a similarity between the responses to the two propositions in that in both cases there are two fairly well supported (and fairly equally supported) categories, and three other categories containing significant, though lower, proportions of respondents. It is this similarity which results in the entropy value being almost the same for the two propositions.

Moving down the list, a comparison of propositions 4 and 14 is also instructive. To the proposition that 'privatisation will not reduce production costs unless combined with measures to increase competition', most economists responded by ticking categories A

**Figure 9 (Part II)** $\longrightarrow$

| No. of proposition | Response pattern A B C D E | Overall weight of opinion for or against the proposition | Index of disagreement amongst respondents |
|---|---|---|---|
| 8. The fear of being taken over is a significant force leading managers to increase profits | | +0.5 | 80% |
| 16. The long-run consequences of financing government expenditure by taxation are the same as financing it by borrowing | | -0.7 | 80% |
| 2. A ceiling on rents reduces the quantity and quality of housing available | | +1.0 | 80% |
| 27. Tariffs and import quotas reduce general economic welfare | | +0.8 | 79% |
| 21. Deficiency payments are more efficient instruments of agricultural support than intervention buying | | +0.6 | 78% |
| 15. Government expenditure has a greater domestic stimulatory impact than equivalent tax reduction | | +0.9 | 78% |
| 4. Privatising hitherto publicly owned and operated industries will not reduce production costs unless combined with measures to increase competition | | +1.1 | 76% |
| 14. Non-tariff barriers have a more significant influence on trade flows than tariff barriers | | +0.6 | 75% |
| 35. The redistribution of income in the developed industrial nations is a legitimate task for the government | | +1.3 | 70% |
| 13. In the short run, unemployment can be reduced by accepting an increase in the rate of inflation | | +0.8 | 69% |
| 10. Fiscal policy has a significant stimulative impact on a less than fully employed economy | | +1.1 | 68% |
| 5. Regulating the price of agricultural products above competitive market levels results in surpluses | | +1.5 | 53% |

# Figure 9 (Part I):
# A summary of responses to the 35 propositions

The chart on the next three pages gives a summary of the responses to the 35 propositions on the questionnaire. The propositions are listed in order of relative entropy, with the highest entropy proposition listed first, the next highest second, and so on. So the propositions at the beginning of the chart are those which produced the greatest amount of disagreement amongst respondents, those at the end of the chart produced the greatest degree of consensus. The number at the beginning of each proposition is the number of the proposition as it appeared on the questionnaire.

## Key

The small bar chart shows the response pattern. The leftmost bar is the 'agree strongly' category (A), next is 'agree with reservations' (B), then 'neither agree nor disagree' (C), 'generally disagree' (D), and finally the rightmost bar is 'disagree strongly' (E). The figures on which the bar charts are based will be found in Part II of this Figure on the reverse side.

-0.1

This shows the mean response score, with each A (agree strongly) response scored as +2, each B response as +1, each C as 0, each D as −1, and each E (disagree strongly) as −2. The mean response score is a measure of the overall weight of opinion in favour (positive mean response score) or against (negative mean response score) the proposition.

95%

Relative entropy, calculated as described in Appendix 2. This is a measure of 'disagreement' amongst respondents. The propositions are listed in the chart in order of decreasing entropy (i.e. increasing consensus).

*Note:* 'How the Economists Responded to the 35 Propositions' (on the reverse of this pull out section).

The figure under each 'tick box' is the percentage opting for that response. Percentages are based on 981 usable replies. They do not sum to exactly 100% because on individual propositions, between 0·2% and 1·8% of respondents failed to tick any box.

16. The long-run consequences of financing government expenditure by taxation are the same as financing it by borrowing

| A | B | C | D | E |
|---|---|---|---|---|
| 2·0 | 14·3 | 14·2 | 51·1 | 17·9 |

17. Cash payments are superior to transfers-in-kind

| A | B | C | D | E |
|---|---|---|---|---|
| 18·9 | 41·0 | 23·3 | 13·3 | 2·8 |

18. The government should restructure the welfare system along lines of a 'negative income tax'

| A | B | C | D | E |
|---|---|---|---|---|
| 22·9 | 45·9 | 15·5 | 11·9 | 3·4 |

19. Effluent taxes represent a better approach to pollution control than imposition of pollution ceilings

| A | B | C | D | E |
|---|---|---|---|---|
| 19·1 | 39·7 | 15·7 | 18·5 | 6·0 |

20. 'Consumer protection' laws generally reduce economic efficiency

| A | B | C | D | E |
|---|---|---|---|---|
| 4·4 | 13·6 | 21·4 | 41·4 | 18·8 |

21. Deficiency payments are more efficient instruments of agricultural support than intervention buying

| A | B | C | D | E |
|---|---|---|---|---|
| 16·7 | 37·5 | 37·4 | 5·6 | 1·5 |

22. Permitting trade in human organs for transplant purposes would be economically efficient

| A | B | C | D | E |
|---|---|---|---|---|
| 6·9 | 30·0 | 24·4 | 17·4 | 19·5 |

23. The government should take stronger powers to control takeover activities

| A | B | C | D | E |
|---|---|---|---|---|
| 19·5 | 35·3 | 23·2 | 17·5 | 3·8 |

24. Antitrust laws should be used vigorously to reduce monopoly power from its current level

| A | B | C | D | E |
|---|---|---|---|---|
| 24·4 | 39·8 | 20·7 | 12·0 | 2·5 |

25. Financial markets are inefficient because short-term returns are the dominant influence, and long-term consequences are relatively neglected

| A | B | C | D | E |
|---|---|---|---|---|
| 24·0 | 39·9 | 13·7 | 17·1 | 4·9 |

26. The power of the trade unions is not a significant economic problem

| A | B | C | D | E |
|---|---|---|---|---|
| 10·1 | 33·1 | 17·7 | 30·7 | 8·0 |

27. Tariffs and import quotas reduce general economic welfare

| A | B | C | D | E |
|---|---|---|---|---|
| 24·9 | 49·1 | 11·7 | 11·6 | 1·8 |

28. The money supply is a more important target than interest rates for monetary policy

| A | B | C | D | E |
|---|---|---|---|---|
| 6·8 | 22·3 | 27·8 | 32·0 | 10·2 |

29. The distribution of income in the developed industrial nations should be more equal

| A | B | C | D | E |
|---|---|---|---|---|
| 32·6 | 33·5 | 20·0 | 9·8 | 3·3 |

30. Wage-price controls should be used to control inflation

| A | B | C | D | E |
|---|---|---|---|---|
| 5·4 | 28·3 | 14·4 | 30·1 | 21·2 |

31. The central bank should be instructed to increase the money supply at a fixed rate

| A | B | C | D | E |
|---|---|---|---|---|
| 3·1 | 13·6 | 28·0 | 37·4 | 17·2 |

32. The European Monetary System offers a superior mechanism to a regime of floating exchange rates

| A | B | C | D | E |
|---|---|---|---|---|
| 19·2 | 46·6 | 16·6 | 12·6 | 4·5 |

33. The prime concern of macro-economic policy should be to eliminate inflation

| A | B | C | D | E |
|---|---|---|---|---|
| 4·9 | 16·7 | 14·2 | 40·4 | 23·2 |

34. The level of government spending should be reduced (disregarding expenditures for stabilisation)

| A | B | C | D | E |
|---|---|---|---|---|
| 6·6 | 11·9 | 15·1 | 34·0 | 31·9 |

35. The redistribution of income in the developed industrial nations is a legitimate task for the government

| A | B | C | D | E |
|---|---|---|---|---|
| 49·5 | 36·6 | 5·9 | 3·8 | 3·6 |

| No. of proposition | Response pattern A B C D E | Overall weight of opinion for or against the proposition | Index of disagreement amongst respondents |
|---|---|---|---|

22. Permitting trade in human organs would be economically efficient — −0.1 — 95%

30. Wage-price controls should be used to control inflation — −0.3 — 92%

28. The money supply is a more important target than interest rates for monetary policy — −0.2 — 92%

11. Inflation is primarily a monetary phenomenon — +0.0 — 92%

26. The power of the trade unions is not a significant economic problem — +0.1 — 91%

19. Effluent taxes represent a better approach to pollution control than imposition of pollution ceilings — +0.5 — 91%

23. The government should take stronger powers to control takeover activities — +0.5 — 91%

34. The level of government spending should be reduced (disregarding expenditures for stabilisation) — −0.7 — 90%

25. Financial markets are inefficient because short-term returns are the dominant influence, and long-term consequences are relatively neglected — +0.6 — 89%

33. The prime concern of macroeconomic policy should be to eliminate inflation — −0.6 — 89%

9. Replacement of domestic rates by the Community Charge will increase the price of owner-occupied housing — +0.5 — 89%

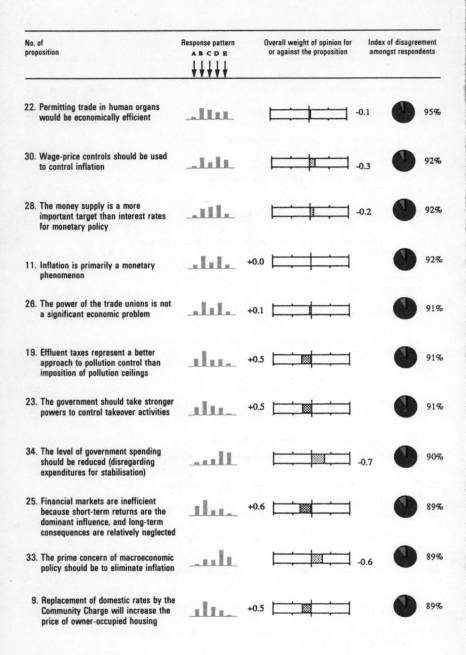

| No. of proposition | Response pattern ABCDE | Overall weight of opinion for or against the proposition | Index of disagreement amongst respondents |
|---|---|---|---|
| 20. 'Consumer protection' laws generally reduce economic efficiency | | -0.6 | 88% |
| 31. The central bank should be instructed to increase the money supply at a fixed rate | | -0.5 | 88% |
| 29. The distribution of income in the developed industrial nations should be more equal | | +0.8 | 87% |
| 7. The regulatory authorities will ensure that prices are lower in the Gas and Telecommunications industries than they would have been in the absence of regulation | | +0.3 | 87% |
| 17. Cash payments are superior to transfers-in-kind | | +0.6 | 86% |
| 24. Antitrust laws should be used vigorously to reduce monopoly power from its current level | | +0.7 | 86% |
| 32. The European Monetary System offers a superior mechanism to a regime of floating exchange rates | | +0.6 | 85% |
| 1. A minimum wage increases unemployment among young and unskilled workers | | +0.6 | 84% |
| 18. The government should restructure the welfare system along lines of a 'negative income tax' | | +0.7 | 84% |
| 12. The central bank has the capacity to achieve a constant rate of growth of the money supply if it is so desired | | -0.5 | 84% |
| 6. Ceteris paribus, a shift from a fault system to 'no fault' divorce will result in an increase in the quantity of divorce | | +0.7 | 83% |
| 3. The fundamental cause of the rise in oil prices in the 1970s was the monopoly power of the Organisation of Oil Exporting Countries (OPEC) | | +0.8 | 82% |

# Figure 9 (Part II):
## How the economists responded to the 35 propositions

Please tick one box for each proposition:

| A☐ | B☐ | C☐ | D☐ | E☐ |
|---|---|---|---|---|
| Agree strongly | Agree with reservations | Neither agree nor disagree | Generally disagree | Disagree strongly |

1. A minimum wage increases unemployment among young and unskilled workers

    A☐ B☐ C☐ D☐ E☐
    20·1 48·5 9·5 15·2 6·2

2. A ceiling on rents reduces the quantity and quality of housing available

    A☐ B☐ C☐ D☐ E☐
    34·1 43·7 8·8 9·5 3·4

3. The fundamental cause of the rise in oil prices in the 1970s was the monopoly power of the Organisation of Petroleum Exporting Countries (OPEC)

    A☐ B☐ C☐ D☐ E☐
    26·8 46·4 9·7 12·6 3·8

4. Privatising hitherto publicly owned and operated industries will not reduce production costs unless combined with measures to increase competition

    A☐ B☐ C☐ D☐ E☐
    46·0 34·5 7·5 9·7 1·7

5. Regulating the price of agricultural products above competitive market levels results in surpluses

    A☐ B☐ C☐ D☐ E☐
    62·5 32·2 3·0 1·5 0·6

6. Ceteris paribus, a shift from a fault system to 'no fault' divorce law will result in an increase in the quantity of divorce

    A☐ B☐ C☐ D☐ E☐
    21·6 35·6 31·8 7·7 1·5

7. The regulatory authorities will ensure that prices are lower in the Gas and Telecommunication industries than they would have been in the absence of regulation

    A☐ B☐ C☐ D☐ E☐
    9·9 39·0 27·5 19·3 3·9

8. The fear of being taken over is a significant force leading managers to increase profits

    A☐ B☐ C☐ D☐ E☐
    10·2 49·2 23·3 14·5 2·3

9. Replacement of domestic rates by the Community Charge will increase the price of owner-occupied housing

    A☐ B☐ C☐ D☐ E☐
    18·1 37·4 25·2 15·1 3·5

10. Fiscal policy has a significant stimulative impact on a less than fully employed economy

    A☐ B☐ C☐ D☐ E☐
    28·4 55·9 9·2 5·3 0·7

11. Inflation is primarily a monetary phenomenon

    A☐ B☐ C☐ D☐ E☐
    9·7 32·2 16·5 31·8 9·3

12. The central bank has the capacity to achieve a constant rate of growth of the money supply if it is so desired

    A☐ B☐ C☐ D☐ E☐
    4·0 18·8 11·9 48·4 16·5

13. In the short run, unemployment can be reduced by accepting an increase in the rate of inflation

    A☐ B☐ C☐ D☐ E☐
    14·0 62·7 11·0 10·6 1·5

14. Non-tariff barriers have a more significant influence on trade flows than tariff barriers

    A☐ B☐ C☐ D☐ E☐
    12·5 39·4 40·4 6·3 0·6

15. Government expenditure has a greater domestic stimulatory impact than equivalent tax reduction

    A☐ B☐ C☐ D☐ E☐
    27·7 48·3 13·5 8·6 1·5

or B. The balance of opinion is very favourable to this proposition and the mean response score is 1·1. Only two other propositions (on the effects of agricultural price regulation and the legitimacy of government attempts to redistribute income) produced a more decisive balance of opinion. To the proposition (number 14) that 'non-tariff barriers have a more significant impact on trade flows than tariff barriers', most economists responded by ticking categories B or C. The result is a balance of opinion which is clearly in agreement but much less decisively so than is the case for proposition 4. The mean response score is 0·6, only just over one-half of that for proposition 4. But the two propositions have almost the same relative entropy score. In each case there are two heavily supported categories, two with minor support, and one category with virtually no support.

## Effects of combining response categories

It will be recalled that earlier surveys used fewer response categories, and it was not clear whether the ranking of propositions would be greatly changed if some of our categories were amalgamated and the entropy figures recalculated. Accordingly, another ranking was calculated based upon three categories—A and B combined (agree), C (don't know), and D and E combined (disagree). Because of the asymmetrical nature of the response categories used in earlier surveys, a further ranking was tried using four categories—A, B, C, and D + E. Some startling changes can occur in the rankings when this is done. An extreme example is proposition 34 which has the eighth highest relative entropy in Figure 9, but has a lower relative entropy than all but three of the propositions when four categories are used. Other examples are more reassuring. Proposition 5 always has the lowest relative entropy, while proposition 23 is always among those with the highest entropy. In Appendix 2 we report all three rankings and the correlations between them.

In addition to relative entropy, the standard deviation of responses to each proposition was calculated using the scoring system detailed above. The standard deviation clearly does take account of the 'distance' between response categories and would produce a higher figure for polarised opinion than for opinion divided between adjacent categories. This provided us with a rough check on whether use of the entropy measure was likely to produce systematically different results compared with a reasonable though quite different alternative. The results in Appendix 2 were reassuring in producing a ranking of propositions highly correlated with the ranking by relative entropy.

If asked to guess which propositions would produce the highest and lowest levels of relative entropy, we would have predicted that trade in human organs and the effect of price control on agricultural surpluses would have been at opposite ends of Figure 9. These results are relatively unsurprising. A more detailed consideration of Figure 9, however, requires that we compare the ranking with that obtained in earlier surveys, and consider whether certain types of proposition produce more disagreement than others.

## C. Comparisons with Other Studies

Twenty propositions in our survey were either the same as, or sufficiently close to, those used in earlier surveys to be directly comparable.

### (i) Comparisons of Relative Entropy

Correlations between the relative entropy scores computed by other surveys and those computed from our own survey are reported in Appendix 2. In general (though not in all cases), the correlations are positive, but many are low and not statistically significantly different from zero. On this evidence it seems that the propositions which cause the greatest division between economists are not the same in all countries. A closer investigation, however, reveals some interesting features of the survey results which somewhat mitigate this conclusion.

Comparing the ranking of the 20 propositions common to Kearl's survey and to our own, the Spearman coefficient of rank correlation[1] is 0·31, some way short of the 0·38 required for statistical significance (one-sided test of the hypothesis of no correlation) at the customary 5% level. The full comparison of rankings is given in Table 2. Note that, for the purposes of comparison, propositions ranked first are those with *relatively low* entropy. Thus, our proposition 10 that 'fiscal policy has a significant stimulative impact on a less than fully employed economy' produced the highest level of consensus out of the common 20 propositions and is ranked at number 1.

---

[1] The Spearman rank correlation coefficient takes into account only the rank order of the relative entropy scores, not their actual values, and is a 'distribution-free' measure of monotonic correlation (as compared with the perhaps more familiar Pearson correlation coefficient, which measures specifically linear correlation).

**Table 2:**
**Rankings of Propositions by Relative Entropy**
*(Lowest entropy ranked 1, next lowest 2, etc.)*

| Ricketts/ Shoesmith Prop. Nos.: | Ricketts/ Shoesmith Ranking | Kearl Ranking | Block Ranking | Frey Ranking |
|---|---|---|---|---|
| 1 | 9 | 5 | 4 | 11 |
| 2 | 5 | 2 | 1 | 5 |
| 3 | 6 | 7 | 5 | 2 |
| 10 | 1 | 6 | 9 | 7 |
| 11 | 19 | 17 | 14 | 12 |
| 12 | 7 | 10 | 19 | 13 |
| 13 | 2 | 20 | 18 | 17 |
| 17 | 11 | 4 | 8 | 18 |
| 18 | 8 | 8 | 7 | 20 |
| 19 | 16 | 12 | 12 | 19 |
| 20 | 14 | 15 | 11 | 3 |
| 24 | 10 | 11 | 15 | 6 |
| 26 | 17 | 18 | 17 | 10 |
| 27 | 4 | 1 | 2 | 4 |
| 28 | 18 | 14 | 16 | 14 |
| 29 | 12 | 19 | 20 | 16 |
| 30 | 20 | 3 | 3 | 1 |
| 31 | 13 | 9 | 10 | 8 |
| 34 | 15 | 16 | 13 | 15 |
| 35 | 3 | 13 | 6 | 9 |

*Notes:* (a) Ranking of propositions in study by Kearl *et al.* (1979) from Column (3) Table 3, *American Economic Review*, Vol. 69, No. 2, p. 32.

(b) Ranking of propositions in study by Frey *et al.* (1984) from Table 1, *American Economic Review*, Vol. 74, No. 5, p. 988. The ranking refers to the total sample of nations.

(c) Ranking of propositions in study by Block and Walker (1988) from Table 2, *Canadian Public Policy*, Vol. 14, No. 2, pp. 140-41.

Analysing the table of rankings, it is particularly noticeable that two propositions appear almost at opposite ends of Kearl's ranking and ours. Proposition 13 on the short-run Phillips Curve is a low entropy proposition according to our results (ranked number 2), yet in Kearl's survey it produced the greatest disagreement (ranked number 20). Conversely, proposition 30 that 'wage-price controls should be used to control inflation' produced disagreement in our survey (ranked 20) and relative agreement in Kearl's (ranked number 3). Deleting these 'outliers' and recalculating the Spearman correlation coefficient for the remaining 18 propositions yields a figure of 0·71, well in excess of the 0·40 required for statistical significance at the conventional 5% level (one-sided test) when testing the hypothesis of no correlation. Indeed, the rank correlation of 0·71 is beyond the 0·1% level of significance.

**Possible reasons for differences in results**

It is useful to consider possible reasons for the marked difference in results for the two propositions identified above.

o  That a full decade separates the two surveys suggests that events may have changed opinion. However, the fact that Block's more recent survey ranks these propositions similarly to Kearl's is fairly strong evidence against this point of view.

o  Another possibility is that the rewording of proposition 13, to which reference was made in Section 4 (above, p. 29), made a significant impact on respondents. However, the wording of the other 'rogue' proposition (No. 30) was identical in all surveys.

o  A more serious possibility is that the extension of response categories from three to five has consequences which are unpredictable and affects some propositions more than others. For example, in Kearl's survey, 72% of respondents 'generally disagreed' with the proposition that wage-price controls should be used. Only one response category was available to express disagreement in any form, and there was no opportunity to remain uncommitted (other than by failing to respond). This concentration of responses produced the low entropy result. In the case of the IEA survey there were no less than three alternatives which permitted the expression of reactions less favourable than 'agree with reservations', compared with the single option in Kearl's work. The result was that 66% of respondents distributed themselves over these alternatives and a high entropy figure was produced.

o  If the risk of quirky results deriving from differences in the structure of the IEA survey compared with earlier ones is discounted, we are left with the conclusion that opinion in the UK is indeed structured differently from that in the USA and elsewhere, at least on some crucial issues. There does appear to be a fairly pronounced concentration of opinion accepting the proposition that unemployment can be reduced in the short run at the expense of an increase in the rate of inflation. In the USA,

## Table 3:
## International Comparisons of Economic Opinion

| Proposition Number | U.S.A. (1979) | Austria (1984) | France (1984) | Germany (1984) *(per cent)* | Switz. (1984) | Canada (1988) | U.K. (1989) |
|---|---|---|---|---|---|---|---|
| 1. Agree | 88 | 64 | 38 | 69 | 66 | 85 | 76 |
| Disagree | 10 | 35 | 60 | 30 | 32 | 15 | 24 |
| 2. Agree | 96 | 89 | 52 | 93 | 79 | 95 | 85 |
| Disagree | 2 | 11 | 44 | 6 | 20 | 5 | 14 |
| 20. Agree | 50 | 29 | 22 | 35 | 44 | 46 | 23 |
| Disagree | 46 | 70 | 77 | 65 | 56 | 52 | 77 |
| 27. Agree | 95 | 86 | 70 | 94 | 87 | 96 | 84 |
| Disagree | 3 | 13 | 27 | 6 | 10 | 4 | 15 |
| 30. Agree | 28 | 47 | 54 | 7 | 39 | 26 | 39 |
| Disagree | 71 | 52 | 43 | 92 | 61 | 73 | 60 |
| 35. Agree | 78 | 88 | 88 | 79 | 70 | 84 | 91 |
| Disagree | 19 | 11 | 11 | 21 | 28 | 15 | 8 |

responses were spread much more evenly over the available range. British opinion appears less influenced by the 'rational expectations' thinking of the later 1970s and early 1980s and is more conventionally 'Keynesian'. Only 23% failed to express some form of agreement with proposition 13 (i.e. the 23% includes the 'neither agree nor disagree' category and the few who failed to tick any category) compared with 36% expressing general disagreement in the USA.

## (ii) Comparisons of General Opinion

In subsection (i) our aim was to discuss differences in the amount of disagreement associated with the various propositions in the IEA survey compared with earlier studies. Here we simply compare strength of opinion on particular issues across a range of countries. As was noted in Section 2, Frey *et al.* argued that the countries covered in their study fell into two categories— the USA, Germany and Switzerland on the one hand, and France and Austria on the other. They singled out nine questions of particular importance to this conclusion, six of which appear unchanged in the IEA survey. By combining response categories A and B in Frey's survey into a single class labelled 'agree' the results recorded in Table 3 are obtained. A similar procedure applied to Block's results yields the figures for Canada. The UK column is produced by allocating the 'don't knows' between 'agree' and 'disagree' in proportion to the ratio $(A + B) \div (D + E)$.

Table 3 contains some interesting features of British professional opinion compared with that overseas. Propositions 1 and 2, for example, are concerned with predictions about market behaviour. The UK sample has the highest proportion of respondents in Europe agreeing to the proposition that minimum wages increase unemployment—76% when those who 'neither agree nor disagree' have been re-allocated (69% before re-allocation), compared with 38% in France and 69% in Germany. On this issue opinion in the UK seems to be as close to American norms as to European ones, and these findings would be consistent with the existence of some conflict between Continental European economists and British ones over such issues as European social legislation.

On the effects of rent control, German, Austrian, and Swiss economists take a view comparable with that in the UK though distinctly less 'robust' than that apparent in the USA and Canada. French economists are completely out of line with barely a majority agreeing with the proposition.

### UK economists more in favour of redistributive role for government

Attitudes to the government's role as a redistributor of income are explored in proposition 35. Here it is revealing that the proportion supporting a redistributive role for government is higher in the UK than in any other country (91% after re-allocation of those who 'neither agree nor disagree'). Even the French have a smaller proportion agreeing with proposition 35 than the British. The association, noted by Frey, between national attitudes to the price system and attitudes to government intervention is not borne out by our data. British economists seem to combine a respect for the power of price signals (perhaps gleaned from their American textbooks or from the continuing tradition in micro-economics nourished in post-war years by the IEA), with a clear acceptance of the redistributive role of government, and with a relatively optimistic view of the benign influence of government intervention.

On consumer protection laws (proposition 20), for example, over three-quarters of respondents (after re-allocation of the 'neither agree nor disagree' category) disagreed that such laws reduced economic efficiency—a similar proportion to the French survey, and higher than any of the other countries surveyed. On the other hand, 84% agreed (again after re-allocation of category C respondents) that tariffs and import quotas reduce economic welfare (proposition 27)—a similar proportion to that found in Switzerland and Austria though substantially short of the figures for Germany, Canada and the United States which are a further 10 percentage points higher. The interventionist credentials of French economists are again confirmed by a majority support for the use of wage-price controls (proposition 30). The UK on this issue is positioned mid-way between the French end of the spectrum and the Canadian and US position. German economists are even more clearly opposed to price controls than their American colleagues with a mere 7% agreeing that they should be used to control inflation.

## D. Normative and Positive Propositions

Any attempt to investigate whether opinion is more divided on normative than on positive propositions requires us to identify clearly into which category each proposition falls. This is more difficult than a passing acquaintance with economic methodology might lead one to expect. As Brittan noted in his study,

'nearly all supposedly value judgements contain some implicit empirical assumption, while most would-be factual assertions contain evaluative overtones'. (p. 61)

Kearl, as we have noted, claimed to have found greater consensus on 'can' than 'should' propositions, but the principles that informed the allocation of propositions between the two categories were far from clear. For example, the statement that 'tariffs and import quotas reduce general economic welfare' (proposition 27) was classed as a 'can' proposition—presumably a statement which involved no ethical judgements. Although we might interpret the proposition as a refutable scientific statement if 'economic welfare' is considered to be a technical term for economists which they all understand in the same way, it is by no means obvious that such an interpretation is reasonable. On the contrary, if ideas of what constitutes 'economic welfare' are varied and depend on individual subjective opinions, the proposition could be interpreted as normative and equivalent to the statement 'tariffs and import quotas are bad'.

Even accepting Kearl's initial classification of proposition 27 as a 'can' statement, it is then somewhat confusing to find proposition 20 that 'consumer protection laws generally reduce economic efficiency' classified as a 'should' statement. The two propositions have almost the same form with the substitution of the word 'efficiency' for the word 'welfare'. Indeed, a case could be made that the term 'efficiency' *is* understood in economics circles in a particular technical sense, and that if any one of these two propositions approaches a scientific statement it is number 20 on consumer protection rather than number 27 on tariffs. We would suggest, however, that both propositions should fall into the same category, and that they both contain 'evaluative overtones' which distinguish them from purely factual or predictive statements.

## Status of some propositions debatable

Disputes about the precise status of the propositions contained in the survey are unlikely to be settled easily. Our own preferred solution is to view the first 16 propositions on the questionnaire as 'positive' and the final 19 propositions as 'normative'. Doubts about the treatment of propositions referring to 'efficiency' led us to repeat the analysis reclassifying these in the 'positive' group to see whether our results were greatly affected. This alternative procedure led, for example, to proposition 22 on the efficiency of trade in human organs being re-classified as 'non-normative'. Indeed, there is evidence that at least some respondents interpreted it in this way. A written comment on one returned questionnaire indicated total opposition to trade in human organs on the grounds that it was immoral, whilst accepting that it would be 'economically efficient'.

If we record the rank of each proposition as measured by its entropy score and list the rankings under the headings 'normative' and 'non-normative', the following results, recorded in Table 4, are obtained. The ranking is again from low entropy to high entropy (lowest entropy ranked 1, next lowest 2, and so on).

Applying a Mann-Whitney test (a 'distribution-free' test that is sensitive to a difference in 'average' value between two distributions), we find that the sum of the ranks of the non-normative propositions (195) is much lower than would be expected on the basis of the null hypothesis that entropy is distributed similarly in normative as in non-normative propositions. The probability of a rank sum as or more extreme than that observed, if the null hypothesis is true, is only about 2 in 1,000. There *does* seem to be evidence here that purely predictive questions give rise to less dispersion of opinion than others. The results of the IEA survey therefore lend some support to Kearl's conclusions, and favour Thurow's and Samuelson's rather than Friedman's conjecture about the sources of disagreement in economics discussed in

**Table 4:**
**The Ranks by Relative Entropy of Normative and Non-normative Propositions**

| Normative Propositions | Non-Normative Propositions |
|:---:|:---:|
| 4 | 1 |
| 8 | 2 |
| 9 | 3 |
| 16 | 5 |
| 18 | 6 |
| 19 | 7 |
| 20 | 10 |
| 22 | 11 |
| 23 | 12 |
| 24 | 13 |
| 25 | 14 |
| 27 | 15 |
| 28 | 17 |
| 29 | 21 |
| 30 | 26 |
| 31 | 33 |
| 32 | |
| 34 | |
| 35 | |

Section 1. This conclusion survives the re-classification of propositions 20, 21, 22, 25, and 27 as non-normative. In this case there are 14 normative and 21 non-normative propositions. The significance level of the revised rank sums is still only 4 in 1,000.

### E. Macro *vs* Micro Propositions

Dividing the questionnaire into micro and macro sections is probably less contentious than the normative-positive dichotomy, although even here the selection can present difficulties. Proposition 26 on the power of the trade unions, for example, might be interpreted macro-economically (for instance, the effects of the unions on inflation and unemployment) or micro-economically (for example, their consequences for the operation of particular industries). The reference to an 'economic problem' in the proposition leaves the respondent with a wide freedom of interpretation. We have taken the micro-economic propositions as including numbers 1 to 9 and numbers 17 to 27, and the macro-economic propositions as comprising the remainder. Thus, according to this classification there are 20 micro-economic and 15 macro-economic propositions.

Applying the same procedures as before and recording the rank of each proposition according to its relative entropy score, the sum of the ranks of the macro-economic propositions and the sum of the ranks of the micro-economic propositions were calculated. The rank sums did not differ sufficiently for us to conclude that micro-economic propositions were associated with lower entropy than macro-economic ones. Unlike Kearl, therefore, we found no evidence that the level of consensus was greater in the sphere of micro-economics than in macro-economics.

The results of these relatively simple non-parametric statistical techniques were confirmed by a two-way analysis of variance using the micro/macro and positive/normative dichotomies as the two factors in the analysis. The unbalanced split of propositions between the two dichotomies, and possible interactions between the factors, can be explicitly taken into account in such an analysis. The difference between the mean entropy level for positive and normative propositions was strongly significant, whereas that between micro and macro propositions was small and not statistically significant.

# SEVEN

# Vested Interests, Experience and Opinion

In this section we investigate the relationships between responses to the various propositions, and the demographic and other information requested in the first part of the questionnaire. Figure 10 summarises the results of these analyses by indicating the degree of statistical significance attached to relationships between the responses to each proposition and the age, sex, highest qualification, employment category and specialisation of the respondent.

There are two sets of results. The first is based upon simple two-way cross-tabulations and the chi-squared 'goodness-of-fit' statistic. A statistically significant result from this statistic in a two-way cross-tabulation is an indication that the two variables defining the cross-tabulation are not independent of each other. Most of the discussion below uses these results. The second set of results attempts to take account of the simultaneous influence of several demographic factors. As was seen in Section 5, there are statistically significant relationships between age and employment, sex and specialisation, employment and sex, and so on. It was therefore necessary to check whether, for example, the observation of a connection between employment and attitudes to the distribution of income (proposition 29) was deceptive and might rather have reflected the indirect influence of age or specialisation or sex via the correlation of one or more of these latter variables with employment type.

The modelling technique we used was a 'backward elimination' method which begins with a model involving several factors and their interactions. The model is then progressively simplified by eliminating terms, one by one, if they are shown to have no additional statistically significant explanatory power in the presence of all other factors and interactions included in the model at that stage of testing. The factors that survive this process, for each proposition, are shown in the right-hand part of Figure 10. As can be seen from the table, the general pattern of relationships is

# Figure 10:
## Significant relationships between personal characteristics and responses to the 35 propositions

| | Results from two-way cross-tabulation | | | | | Results from multi-factor modelling | | | | |
| --- | :---: | :---: | :---: | :---: | :---: | :---: | :---: | :---: | :---: | :---: |
| | Age ▲ | Sex ● | Qualification ◆ | Employment ■ | Specialisation ▼ | Age ▲ | Sex ● | Qualification ◆ | Employment ■ | Specialisation ▼ |
| 1. A minimum wage increases unemployment among young and unskilled workers | △ | | | □ | | △ | | | ■ | |
| 2. A ceiling on rents reduces the quantity and quality of housing available | ▲ | | ◇ | | | ▲ | | | ■ | |
| 3. The fundamental cause of the rise in oil prices in the 1970s was the monopoly power of the Organisation of Oil Exporting Countries (OPEC) | △ | | ◇ | | | △ | | | | ▽ |
| 4. Privatising hitherto publicly owned and operated industries will not reduce production costs unless combined with measures to increase competition | | | | | | | | | □ | |
| 5. Regulating the price of agricultural products above competitive market levels results in surpluses | | | ◆ | | | | | | | ▽ |
| 6. Ceteris paribus, a shift from a fault system to "no fault" divorce will result in an increase in the quantity of divorce | | | | | | | | | | |
| 7. The regulatory authorities will ensure that prices are lower in the Gas and Telecommunications industries than they would have been in the absence of regulation | | | | | | | | | □ | |
| 8. The fear of being taken over is a significant force leading managers to increase profits | | | | | | | | | | |
| 9. Replacement of domestic rates by the Community charge will increase the price of owner-occupied housing | | | | | | | | | | |
| 10. Fiscal policy has a significant stimulative impact on a less than fully employed economy | | | | ■ | | | | | ■ | |
| 11. Inflation is primarily a monetary phenomenon | | ● | | | | | ○ | | | |
| 12. The central bank has the capacity to achieve a constant rate of growth of the money supply if it is so desired | | ○ | | □ | ▼ | | | | | ▼ |
| 13. In the short run, unemployment can be reduced by accepting an increase in the rate of inflation | | ● | | | | | ○ | | | |
| 14. Non-tariff barriers have a more significant influence on trade flows than tariff barriers | △ | | | | ▼ | △ | | | | ▼ |
| 15. Government expenditure has a greater domestic stimulatory impact than equivalent tax reduction | | | | ■ | | | | | ■ | |
| 16. The long-run consequences of financing government expenditure by taxation are the same as financing it by borrowing | | | | ▽ | | | | | □ | |

| | statistically significant relationship beyond the 5% level of significance |
| --- | --- |
| △ ○ ◇ □ ▽ | statistically significant relationship beyond the 5% level of significance |
| ◭ ◔ ◈ ◪ ▾ | statistically significant relationship beyond the 1% level of significance |
| ▲ ● ◆ ■ ▼ | statistically significant relationship beyond the 0·1% level of significance |

The results for the two-way tabulations are based on the Pearson chi-squared statistic, those for the multi-factor log-linear modelling are based on the likelihood ratio statistic.

| | Results from two-way cross-tabulation | | | | | Results from multi-factor modelling | | | | |
| --- | :---: | :---: | :---: | :---: | :---: | :---: | :---: | :---: | :---: | :---: |
| | Age ▲ | Sex ● | Qualification ◆ | Employment ■ | Specialisation ▼ | Age ▲ | Sex ● | Qualification ◆ | Employment ■ | Specialisation ▼ |
| 17. Cash payments are superior to transfers-in-kind | | | ◇ | | | | | | | |
| 18. The government should restructure the welfare system along lines of a "negative income tax" | | | | | | | | | | |
| 19. Effluent taxes represent a better approach to pollution control than imposition of pollution ceilings | | | | | | | | | | |
| 20. "Consumer protection" laws generally reduce economic efficiency | | | ◇ | □ | | | | ◈ | | |
| 21. Deficiency payments are more efficient instruments of agricultural support than intervention buying | | | | | ▾ | | ○ | | | ▾ |
| 22. Permitting trade in human organs would be economically efficient | | ◔ | ◇ | | | | ○ | ◇ | | |
| 23. The government should take stronger powers to control takeover activities | | | | □ | | | | | □ | |
| 24. Antitrust laws should be used vigorously to reduce monopoly power from its current level | | | | | | | | ◇ | | |
| 25. Financial markets are inefficient because short-term returns are the dominant influence, and long-term consequences are relatively neglected | | ◔ | | | | | ● | | | |
| 26. The power of the trade unions is not a significant economic problem | ◭ | | | | | | | | | |
| 27. Tariffs and import quotas reduce general economic welfare | | | | | | | | | | |
| 28. The money supply is a more important target than interest rates for monetary policy | | ○ | | ◪ | ▽ | | | | ◪ | ▽ |
| 29. The distribution of income in the developed industrial nations should be more equal | ◭ | ○ | | ◪ | ▾ | ◭ | | | ◪ | ▾ |
| 30. Wage-price controls should be used to control inflation | | ○ | | ◪ | ▽ | | ○ | | ◪ | |
| 31. The central bank should be instructed to increase the money supply at a fixed rate | | ◔ | | | | | ◔ | | | |
| 32. The European Monetary System offers a superior mechanism to a regime of floating exchange rates | | ○ | | | ▽ | | ○ | | | ▾ |
| 33. The prime concern of macro economic policy should be to eliminate inflation | | ○ | | □ | | | ◔ | | ◪ | |
| 34. The level of government spending should be reduced (disregarding expenditures for stabilisation) | | ○ | | □ | | | ○ | | □ | |
| 35. The redistribution of income in the developed industrial nations is a legitimate task for the government | | ◔ | | ◪ | | | ◔ | | ◪ | |

modified but not fundamentally changed by this analysis, as compared with the results in the left-hand half of Figure 10.

## (i) Employment

Of the 35 propositions, 12 yield significantly different response patterns by employment category in two-way cross-tabulations (at the 5% significance level or beyond). Figure 11 indicates broadly how nine of these response patterns differ by summing the two 'agree' categories and the two 'disagree' categories and simply omitting the 'don't knows'. For 10 out of the 12 propositions, employment was indicated as a significant influence on response pattern also by the multi-factor modelling. The exceptions were proposition 12, concerning the central bank's capacity to achieve a constant rate of growth of the money supply, and proposition 20, on the economic efficiency of consumer protection laws.

The opinion of government economists and business economists is distributed differently from that of economists in education with respect to the effect of a minimum wage on unemployment. Nearly a quarter (24%) of academic economists disagreed that a minimum wage increases unemployment, compared with only 12% of government economists and 16% of business economists. Another surprising result was that government economists were more likely to agree that the community charge will increase the price of housing than academic economists (68% compared with 52%).

A larger proportion of business economists agreed that the central bank has the power to control the quantity of money than was the case in education or government (proposition 12), though the multi-factor modelling suggested that this may be at least partly due to the indirect influence of other variables. Business economists were also substantially out of line with their colleagues over the relative impact of tax cuts and government expenditure. Almost one-quarter of business respondents disagreed with the proposition that government expenditure has a greater stimulatory impact than tax cuts (proposition 15).

Business economists also took a notably different view from academics over propositions 20 and 23 on consumer protection and the control of take-overs. A much higher percentage of business economists was prepared to accept the proposition that consumer protection reduces efficiency (31%) compared with academics (16%), although, as with proposition 12, the multi-factor modelling did not confirm the picture given by the simple two-way cross-tabulation. The highest percentage of those opposing extra controls on take-overs occurred among the business economists.

# Figure 11:
# Responses to selected propositions, classified by employment of respondent

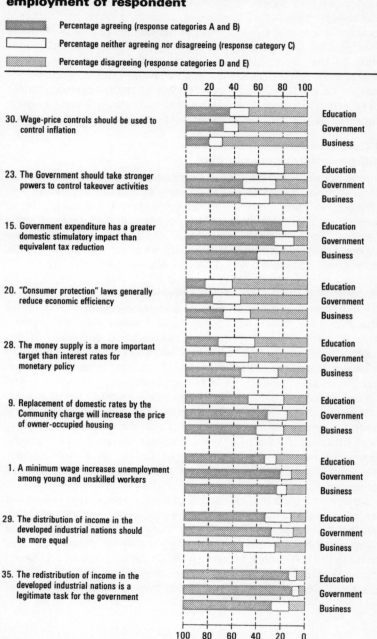

On macro-economic policy issues the differences among employment groups were even more pronounced. The relative importance of a money supply target compared with an interest rate target (proposition 28) was supported by a larger proportion of business economists (46%) than of academics (27%) or of those employed by government. As might have been expected, opposition to the proposition was most pronounced in government employment (48%). On the question of wage-price controls (proposition 30), the business economists were notably opposed (almost 70%). Not a single business economist recorded a 'strongly agree' response to the proposition that such controls should be used.

## Differences between business and government economists

Propositions 29 and 35 on the distribution of income and the role of government again reveal the business economists expressing different opinions from the other employment categories. Here, however, it is with the government economists that the contrast is greatest. For example, only 10% of government employees opposed the proposition that the distribution of income should be more equal compared with 25% of business economists.

## Comparison with Kearl's US results

These results are in some respects comparable with Kearl's in the USA. His study found that academic economists revealed opinions of a different pattern from those employed in business. Of the questions common to both surveys, all those highlighted by Kearl as being associated with differences of opinion between academic and business economists (mainly over macro-economic policy and the distribution of income) were also those found to result in such differences in the UK, with the exception of proposition 24 on the control of monopoly and proposition 13 on the inflation/unemployment trade-off. As we have seen, however, the proposition on the control of take-overs, which did not appear in Kearl's survey, produced significant divergences of opinion between employment categories in our survey.

Kearl also noted that questions of a micro-economic nature did not produce divergences of opinion between employment categories. It is apparent from Figure 10 that some divergence on micro-economic issues between employment categories *was* found in the IEA survey. Indeed, the multi-factor analysis reinforces this conclusion with five of the nine positive micro-economic questions yielding different responses by employment category at the 5% level of significance or beyond. It is a curious feature of our results that of the micro-economic questions we have designated normative or policy related and not merely predictive, the multi-factor modelling identifies only one as associated with differing responses by employment (proposition 23 on the control of take-overs). Why employment should be related to the responses to predictive propositions but not to normative ones in the micro-economic sphere we have not fathomed. For macro-economic propositions the imbalance is reversed, with normative macro-economic questions resulting in the most pronounced differences in the distribution of responses by employment.

This evidence, while consistent with a vested interests theory of opinion, is far from conclusive. In spite of the resistance of business economists to consumer protection and control of take-overs, they did not take a different view over control of monopoly, short-termism in financial markets, or the role of the unions, which might have been expected if vested interests determine opinion. It might also be considered that opinion will to some extent determine employment rather than the other way about. People pathologically suspicious of market processes are not likely to end up as business economists, but this state of mind has not in the past been notably inimical to academic advancement.

## (ii) Age

A glance at Figure 10 reveals the differences in the way opinion is associated with age, compared with employment. Divergence between age groups is signalled predominantly, and perhaps surprisingly, in the area of micro-economics. Further, the divergence of opinion between age groups is mainly over issues we have defined as *positive*. Of the normative macro-economic propositions, on the other hand, only the statement that income distribution should be more equal yields a strongly significant result. Here agreement to the proposition is much more pronounced among the young, and gradually tails off with advancing years. The proportion of those in their twenties agreeing with the proposition (A + B) was 80%, compared with 55% of respondents in their fifties (Figure 12).

Several conjectures are possible to explain these results. One possibility is that attitudes to income distribution are extremely important and condition responses to so-called 'positive' propositions. People would prefer *not* to believe that a minimum wage will increase unemployment if they are very committed to a policy of redistribution, or that rent control reduces the supply of housing if they are particularly worried about the effect of high rents on poor

# Figure 12:
# Responses to selected propositions, classified by age-group of respondent

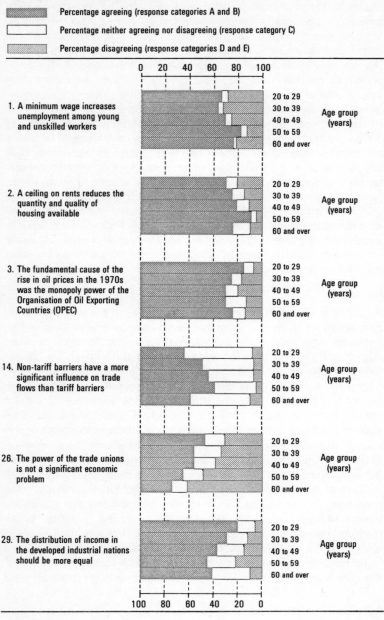

people. This explanation loses some of its force, however, when it is considered that if a desire for income redistribution influences attitudes to positive propositions, it should *a fortiori* influence attitudes to the normative propositions, but little evidence of this could be found. There was, for example, no association between age and support for a negative income tax or hostility to reductions in government spending.

## Age, experience and attitudes

An alternative possibility is that attitudes to the positive micro-economic propositions are conditioned not merely by reading micro-economic theory but also by experience. From this point of view it is notable that many of the propositions leading to diverging opinions between age groups have an historical dimension. For people in their twenties the rented sector of the housing market is something they read about in books on economic or social history, whereas other economists may have spent half a lifetime charting its continual decline. This interpretation gains in plausibility when it is noticed that economists in their twenties are distributed across the 'agree' categories in a different way from older economists. This is something which is hidden in Figure 12 because we have aggregated the 'agree strongly' and 'agree with reservations' categories. For example, while 70% of those in their twenties agreed to the proposition on rent control, 53% did so with reservations. Economists in their fifties by contrast were not only more inclined to agree (90%) but were more evenly spread between the two available categories of agreement (44% agreeing strongly and 46% agreeing with reservations).

Similarly, the OPEC oil crisis of the 1970s was of continual professional interest to one generation of economists, while for very young ones it is probably of only minor significance. The proposition on the unions, the only normative micro-economic question for which age was a significant determinant of response in the simple two-way analyses, might also be seen in an historical perspective. For economists in their twenties and early thirties the unions probably seem to have been on the defensive throughout the period of their educational and professional development. Older economists take time to become convinced that their observations of the 1960s and 1970s are no longer relevant.

The results of the IEA survey do not confirm the findings of Block and Walker with respect to Canadian economists. Block found that the responses to three propositions were particularly related to age. These were money *versus* interest rates (28), cash payments *versus*

# Figure 13:
# Responses to selected propositions, classified by sex of respondent

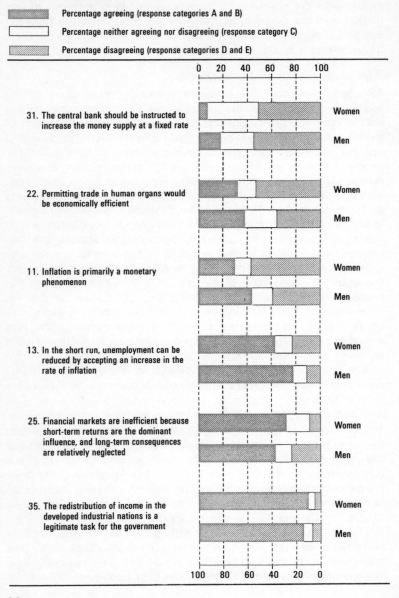

transfers in kind (17), and reductions in the level of government spending (34). As we have seen, none of these propositions produced differing response patterns by age in our sample.

## (iii) Sex

The propositions for which response patterns differed systematically by sex fall predominantly into quite different categories from those for which response patterns differed by age. Figure 10 reveals that no positive micro-economic proposition produced differences in response patterns between sexes at the conventional levels of statistical significance.

On the other hand, *every* normative macro-economic proposition on the questionnaire produced statistically significant differences in the two-way cross-tabulations at the 5% or 1% levels, and five of these eight also emerged in the multi-factor modelling. Differing responses by sex were also apparent in the case of the *positive* macro-economic propositions. Of the total of 13 propositions found to reveal different response patterns by sex in the two-way cross-tabulations, 11 were in macro-economics.

Once again, the IEA survey failed to confirm the results of Block and Walker. For their Canadian sample it was found that the sharpest differences of views between the sexes were over free trade (proposition 27) and the effects of rent control (proposition 2). In the IEA sample no evidence was found to suggest that a similar situation prevails in the UK.

In Figure 13 responses by sex are presented for the six propositions for which the degree of statistical significance exceeds the 1% level. A larger percentage of women than men *disagree* that inflation is a monetary phenomenon (59% compared with 39%). Women are also less inclined to support a money growth rule (proposition 31). The question on attitudes to short-termism in financial markets (proposition 25) revealed a higher proportion of women than men agreeing that these markets were inefficient. The multi-factor analysis confirmed this result at the 0·1% level of significance.

## Strength of women's opposition
## to organ transplant trade

On trade in human organs, women were more likely to express a hostile opinion, although it is interesting that the proportion *agreeing* to the proposition was not so far out of line with that for the men. It appears that a smaller percentage of women were prepared to 'sit on the fence' and that the lower figure (by 10 percentage points) in that category was offset by a similarly higher figure in the 'strongly disagree' category—that is, women who were opposed to the proposition were more *strongly* opposed than were men.

A similar observation applies to female attitudes to income distribution (proposition 35). Here it is noteworthy that the proportions agreeing (A + B) to the proposition that income redistribution is a legitimate task for the government were similar between the sexes. The proportions were 86% and 89% for men and women respectively. However, a full two-thirds of women were *strongly* of this opinion compared with less than half of the men.

# EIGHT

# Expertise and Opinion

## (i) Formal Qualifications

The influence of expertise on opinion was investigated by earlier surveys with varying results. Kearl, for example, broke down the academic respondents into full professors in seven leading graduate programmes and other academic economists. He found significant differences in attitudes between the two employment categories. It is possible to argue, however, that this stratification will not filter out the impact of pure expert opinion but will involve a range of influences including age, qualification, sex, and possibly specialisation. Block and Walker found that for Canadian economists, differences in educational attainment produced very significant differences in response patterns, more striking even than those associated with age or sex. In particular, respondents with a doctorate were more likely

> 'to accept free trade, to be monetarist in their attitude toward monetary policy, to accept the superiority of transfers in cash rather than in kind, . . . to believe that minimum wage laws increase unemployment . . . and that rent controls reduce the quantity and quality of housing available'. (p. 145)

## Disparity of results

The IEA survey of British economists produced results of a quite different character. Figure 10 indicates that, of six propositions associated with differing response patterns by formal qualification in the two-way cross-tabulations, all were micro-economic in character. At first it appears that there is some similarity with Block's survey results. A single macro-economic proposition which reaches the 10% level of significance (not shown in Figure 10) is number 11 on the monetary source of inflation, while the propositions on rent control and cash *versus* in-kind benefits are also significant. Further analysis, however, revealed that these results were attributable to the influence of the group with no formal qualification in economics. When this group was removed, only propositions 18, 20 and 24 were significant at the 5% level and none was significant at the 1% level. All are in the category which we have designated normative and micro-economic. A higher proportion of respondents with doctorates than of those with a master's degree disagreed with the proposition (No. 20) that consumer protection reduces economic efficiency (66% compared with 53%). Respondents with a bachelor's degree were more strongly supportive of the proposition (No. 24) that monopoly power should be reduced than those with a master's degree (71% in agreement compared with 60%). On the negative income tax (proposition 18) the main difference seems to be the larger percentage of those with higher degrees unwilling to make up their minds on the issue.

In general, our survey did not produce much evidence that formal qualifications, at or beyond the level of the bachelor's degree, are associated with opinion on economic propositions. It seems that the first degree in economics in the UK is associated with the sorts of changes in opinion which characterise respondents with doctorates in Canada. It is not clear to us whether we can infer anything about the relative nature of first degrees in Canada and the UK from this evidence, although the British first degree has traditionally been considered to involve more specialised study than is normal in North America.

### (ii) Specialisation and Interest

If we now consider the specialisation column in Figure 10, the importance of macro-economics once more comes to the fore. Confining our discussion to the conventional 1% and 5% levels of significance as in Figure 10, a single micro-economic policy proposition is identified—the proposition that deficiency payments are more efficient than intervention buying as a means of agricultural support. On this question no less than 81% of respondents who identified agriculture and natural resources as their area of specialisation agreed (A + B) with the proposition. In contrast, only 43% of specialists in quantitative economic methods and data, for example, supported the proposition, and 54% of economists as a whole. We conclude that the proposition was indeed a fairly specialised one with which some economists would have been familiar, whilst others were thrown back onto general principles or resorted to the 'don't know' category (which embraced no less than 50% of labour economists).

Turning to the macro-economic propositions, specialists in international economics were more inclined to agree (and to agree more strongly) that non-tariff barriers had a more significant impact on trade flows than tariff barriers. This was a proposition (No. 14) which required knowledge of particular facts and could not be answered by simple appeal to basic theory. It is therefore understandable that specialists in the area would be in a position to take a clearer view on the matter than non-specialists. The other positive macro-economic proposition resulting in differential responses by specialisation in both two-way and multi-factor analyses concerned the power of the central bank to control the money supply (proposition 12). Here 41% of specialists in monetary theory and institutions agreed that the Bank had the power to control the supply of money, if it wished to exercise it, compared with 23% of economists in general. Again the strength of opinion was revealing. Of 159 specialists in labour economics and agriculture and natural resources, not one person agreed strongly with the proposition. This compares with nine of the 78 specialists in monetary theory and institutions.

## Attitudes to income distribution by specialisation

Of the normative macro-economic propositions identified as giving significantly different response patterns by specialisation, the proposition that income distribution should be more equal stands out again as particularly important. Specialists in welfare programmes, consumer economics and urban and regional economics were overwhelmingly in favour of the proposition (80% were in agreement). For those declaring a specialisation in economic growth and development planning 76% agreed, for specialists in quantitative methods 72%, and in industrial structure and organisation 74%. In contrast, specialists in business finance and accounting, international economics, and monetary economics revealed levels of support a full 20 percentage points lower (53, 54, and 55% respectively).

Investigation of the relationship between response patterns and the 'interest' of the respondent largely confirms the results about specialisation. 'Interest' is taken to embrace any of the possible three areas identified by a respondent on the completed questionnaire. The main addition is a noteworthy response pattern for proposition 25 on the dominance of short-term considerations in financial markets. Once again, those expressing an interest in monetary economics and international economics are most opposed to this proposition. On proposition 35 that 'the redistribution of income is a legitimate task for the government', similar results were obtained as described above for proposition 29 and area of specialisation. In general, the levels of support for proposition 35 were higher than those for proposition 29, but the relative disparities between areas of expertise were maintained.

# Predictive Statements and Policy Judgements

As has been discussed in Section 6 (D) of this survey, there is evidence to suggest that the opinion of economists is less dispersed on positive than on normative issues. We still have to inquire, however, if individual attitudes to normative and positive issues are systematically related. Suppose, for example, that economists disagree about policy because they have yet to establish a scientifically robust framework of positive propositions, even though they are broadly united on objectives. Some correlation would then be expected between opinions about predictive statements on the questionnaire and opinions about related policy issues.

## A. Money, Take-Overs and Monopoly Power

As an initial experiment, cross-tabulations were produced of responses to propositions which would be expected to be related. Figure 14, for example, records the responses to proposition 12 (that the central bank has the power to achieve a constant rate of growth in the money supply) against the responses to proposition 28 (that the money supply is a more important target than interest rates for monetary policy). It might be expected that the less confident was the respondent of the capacity of the central bank to control the money supply, the less the reliance which the respondent would place upon the quantity of money in macro-economic policy. Figure 14 reveals that this expected relationship is confirmed. Of those agreeing strongly with proposition 12, 84% agree, or agree with reservations, with proposition 28. Conversely, of those who *disagree* strongly with proposition 12, only 15% agree, or agree with reservations, with proposition 28.

## Positive and normative (policy) attitudes related

Another way of looking at Figure 14 is to note how the modal class changes from one distribution to the next. For those who agree strongly with proposition 12, category A is the most popular

## Figure 14:
## Response patterns for proposition 28, classified by responses to proposition 12

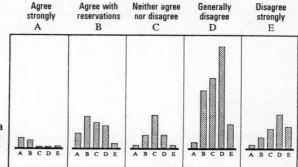

Breakdown by proposition 12:
The central bank has the capacity to achieve a constant rate of growth of the money supply if it is so desired

| Agree strongly A | Agree with reservations B | Neither agree nor disagree C | Generally disagree D | Disagree strongly E |

Response patterns for proposition 28: The money supply is a more important target than interest rates for monetary policy

The diagram shows response patterns for proposition 28, separately for the five groups responding differently to proposition 12. The leftmost panel, for example, shows the response pattern to proposition 28 of those respondents who agreed strongly with proposition 12.

response to proposition 28. For those who pick B as their response to proposition 12, B is the modal response to proposition 28. A choice of C or D for proposition 12 is associated with a modal class of C and D respectively for proposition 28. We have here some rudimentary evidence, therefore, that attitudes to positive propositions and attitudes to normative (policy) propositions are related. It is evidence that can be supplemented by other similar examples.

Figure 15 records the relationship between responses to propositions 8 and 23. If the fear of take-over was seen as a significant force leading managers to increase profits (proposition 8), stronger powers to control take-overs (proposition 23) might be seen as carrying with them adverse consequences for managerial incentives. Some inverse relationship between responses to propositions 8 and 23 would then be expected; it is confirmed by Figure 15. Of those agreeing strongly with proposition 8, 42% disagreed (D + E) with proposition 23. In contrast, of those who generally disagreed with proposition 8, only 14% disagreed with proposition 23. Looking across the figure it is seen that the response pattern to proposition 23 on control of take-overs betrays a high level of entropy (disagreement) for those who agree strongly with proposition 8. A low level of entropy exists for those who

## Figure 15:
## Response patterns for proposition 23, classified by responses to proposition 8

Breakdown by proposition 8:
The fear of being taken over is a significant force
leading managers to increase profits

| Agree strongly A | Agree with reservations B | Neither agree nor disagree C | Generally disagree D | Disagree strongly E |
|---|---|---|---|---|

Response patterns for proposition 23:
The government should take stronger powers to control takeover activities

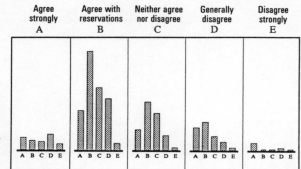

The diagram shows response patterns for proposition 23, separately for the five groups responding differently to proposition 8. The leftmost panel, for example, shows the response pattern to proposition 23 of those respondents who agreed strongly with proposition 8.

## Figure 16:
## Response patterns for proposition 24, classified by responses to proposition 4

Breakdown by response to proposition 4:
Privatising hitherto publicly owned and operated industries
will not reduce production costs unless combined
with measures to increase competition

| Agree strongly A | Agree with reservations B | Neither agree nor disagree C | Generally disagree D | Disagree strongly E |
|---|---|---|---|---|

Response patterns for proposition 24:
Antitrust laws should be used vigorously to reduce monopoly power from its current level

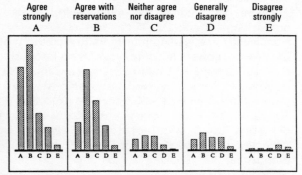

The diagram shows response patterns for proposition 24, separately for the five groups responding differently to proposition 4. The leftmost panel, for example, shows the response pattern to proposition 24 of those respondents who agreed strongly with proposition 4.

72

*disagree* strongly with proposition 8. Proposition 23 is evidently 'easier' to answer (in the affirmative) if some possible adverse effects on managerial incentives are considered to be of little or no practical significance.

A final example of this type of analysis is provided in Figure 16. This relates responses to proposition 4 (that privatisation will not reduce production costs unless combined with measures to stimulate competition) with responses to proposition 24 (that monopoly power should be reduced through the use of anti-trust laws). The hypothesis here is that respondents who reveal a strong opinion that competition is necessary to reduce costs are likely to support a vigorous anti-monopoly policy. This tendency is con-firmed in the table with 75% of those who agree strongly with proposition 4 agreeing (A + B) with proposition 24, compared with only 46% of those who disagree (D + E) with proposition 4.

## B. Wage-Price Controls

Although the idea that differing judgements about empirical issues will be reflected in differing attitudes to policy receives some support from our data, the relationships are far from perfect, and they do not rule out the possibility that value-judgements also play a part in determining responses to the propositions about public policy. Evidence consistent with an important role for ethical judgements can be gleaned from our data. Consider, for example, proposition 30 (which recommends the use of wage-price controls). The correlation coefficient (using response scores ranging from plus 2 for 'agree strongly' to minus 2 for 'disagree strongly') between responses to this proposition, and responses to proposition 1 on the effect of a minimum wage, is negative and significant (−0·39), as Friedman would expect. Presumably the greater the expected impact of a minimum wage on unemployment, the less attractive any policy which attempts to control the level of wages will appear. The more powerful price signals are perceived to be, the more cautious will become the attempts to interfere with them. However, it is also true that the correlation coefficient between responses to proposition 30 and responses to proposition 29 (that the distribution of income should be more equal) is also strongly significant and *positive* (0·48). The more concerned are respondents to achieve a more equal distribution of income the more willing they are to countenance the use of wage-price controls.

In order to investigate the roles of differences in positive analysis and differences in value-judgements in explaining conflicting attitudes to policy, an analysis of the relationships between

## Figure 17:
## Response patterns for proposition 30, 'Wage-price controls should be used to control inflation', cross-classified by responses to propositions 1 and 29

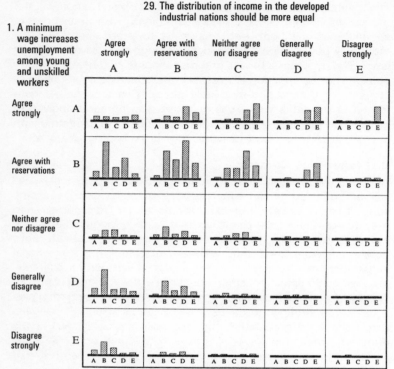

29. The distribution of income in the developed industrial nations should be more equal

1. A minimum wage increases unemployment among young and unskilled workers

responses to propositions 1, 29 and 30 was undertaken. The objective was to see whether, *for any given opinion on the distribution of income*, it was true that support for proposition 1 was associated with hostility to proposition 30, and *for any given opinion on the effect of a minimum wage*, support for proposition 29 was associated with support for proposition 30. The easiest procedure was simply to cross-tabulate responses to the relevant propositions using suitably 'filtered' data. Figure 17 shows the results.

## (i) Samuelson's Conjecture
The idea that economists disagree widely over basic values and that, for any given understanding concerning positive propositions,

therefore, attitudes to policy will be systematically related to ethical judgements, we refer to as 'Samuelson's conjecture' (above, Section 1, p. 24). Consider the top row of Figure 17. All the respondents whose opinions are recorded in that row 'strongly agree' that a minimum wage increases unemployment. However, the respondents may *disagree* about the distribution of income. As we move along the row, opinion becomes more hostile to income redistribution. Associated with this move is a tendency for opinion on the use of wage-price controls to become more opposed until, for those strongly opposed to further income redistribution, respondents are almost unanimous in their opposition to wage-price controls. Relative entropy for the group of respondents in row A, column E, is extremely low on this issue. For the group in row A, column A, relative entropy is extremely high, with all shades of opinion about wage-price controls almost equally represented. In other words, if we know that an economist is strongly opposed to further income redistribution and strongly agrees that minimum wages increase unemployment, we can be very confident that he or she will disagree with wage-price controls. If, however, the economist is known to support strongly further income redistribution, and strongly agrees that minimum wages increase unemployment, it is impossible to predict his or her opinion on wage-price control with any degree of assurance.

## Attitudes to income distribution and public policy

The cross-tabulations upon which the above comments are based are reproduced in Appendix 3, Table A1. Of the 35 people who 'did not disagree' with wage controls (A + B + C) only two expressed disagreement with income redistribution. Of the 97 who strongly opposed wage-price controls, nearly half expressed disagreement with income redistribution. From this evidence, attitudes to the distribution of income play an important role in determining attitudes to public policy. Using the responses of people who disagreed with proposition 1 and doubted that a minimum wage affected employment levels, similar results were obtained, although the statistical significance of the relationships was weaker, as indeed would be expected.

## (ii) Friedman's Conjecture

The idea that economists disagree widely over empirical propositions and that, for any given ethical position, therefore, attitudes to policy will be systematically influenced by attitudes to related positive questions, we refer to as Friedman's conjecture. Looking down column A of Figure 17 we observe the responses of people who 'agree strongly' that the distribution of income should be more equal but who become progressively hostile to the proposition that a minimum wage increases unemployment. Thus we should be observing the impact of differences in attitudes to an empirical proposition alone. Although the effects are somewhat less clear than was the case for Samuelson's conjecture, the tendency for opposition to proposition 1 to be associated with support for wage-price controls is apparent. Thus opposition to wage-price controls (the proportion of responses in categories D and E) fades away as we move down column A. The balance of opinion in rows D or E and column A is the reverse of that in row A and columns D or E.

The cross-tabulation in Appendix 3, Table A2, confirms that attitudes to wage-price controls are not independent of opinions about the effects of a minimum wage. For example, 72% of those who generally disagree with wage-price controls accept (A + B) that a minimum wage increases unemployment. In contrast, only 45% of those who 'agree strongly' with wage-price controls believe that minimum wages have adverse effects on employment. Repeating this experiment using respondents hostile to income redistribution (those that ticked D and E in response to proposition 29) reveals even more significant relationships. This again would be expected since these respondents would presumably see no off-setting distributional advantages to any perceived efficiency losses associated with wage-price controls. Of the 77 respondents who were strongly opposed to wage-price controls and were opposed to a more equal distribution of income, not one opposed (D + E) the proposition that minimum wages increase unemployment.

## Problems of selection and interpretation

In the above analysis an ethical proposition and an empirical proposition are seen to influence the distribution of responses to the policy of wage-price controls. It is worth explicitly considering, however, why the attitude of respondents to the policy of wage-price controls was not uniquely determined by the two selected propositions. There are two obvious factors of relevance here.

First, although we may accept that attitudes to policy will be determined by both empirical and ethical considerations, it is not likely that a mere two propositions will be sufficient to isolate all the significant issues. A great many empirical questions may influence a person's attitude to the use of wage-price controls. By selecting a single proposition to represent the empirical side we have inevitably

**Figure 18:**
**Response patterns for proposition 31, 'The central bank should be instructed to increase the money supply at a fixed rate', cross-classified by responses to propositions 11 and 33**

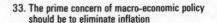
33. The prime concern of macro-economic policy should be to eliminate inflation

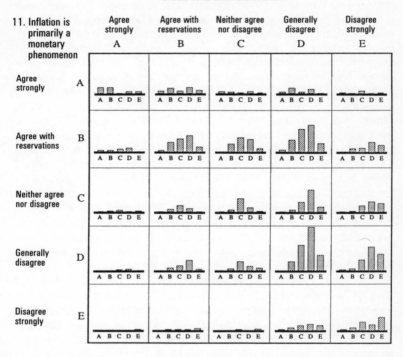

imposed our own *a priori* judgement about the sort of empirical issue which people 'ought' to think of relevance. A broad proposition which reveals a respondent's assessment of the consequences of interfering in the process of wage determination seems a sensible choice to us, but others may disagree and point to empirical issues they consider of greater importance to the determination of attitudes. In other words, we have inevitably made a kind of methodological judgement and imposed it on the analysis.

Secondly, interpretation of the propositions is likely to vary between respondents. What is meant by 'the distribution of income' or the idea of making it 'more equal'? What 'developed industrial nations' had our respondents in mind when they recorded their answers? How 'strongly' did a respondent have to feel before he or she recorded a 'strong' opinion? What kind of 'minimum wage' legislation is implied by proposition 1? How radical are we to assume the interference in wage bargaining to be? These interpretative problems are unavoidably associated with a survey of this type, and differences in interpretation will be expected to produce considerable recorded variations in attitudes to wage-price controls even among people who have recorded the 'same' responses to propositions 1 and 29.

## C. The Money Growth Rule

Responses to proposition 31 (that the money supply should be increased at a fixed rate) were analysed in a similar way to find evidence in support of Friedman's or Samuelson's conjecture. Figure 18 illustrates how the distribution of responses to the proposition on the money growth rule was related to opinion on other issues. Along the rows opinion becomes increasingly hostile to the anti-inflation objective. Down the columns opinion becomes more opposed to the idea that inflation is primarily a monetary phenomenon. Support for Friedman's conjecture requires the proportion of respondents supporting the money growth rule to change as we move up or down the columns. Support for Samuelson's conjecture would be associated with a change in the distribution of responses to the money growth rule as we move along the rows.

There is some statistical evidence for both effects (Tables A3 and A4 in Appendix 3), although the small number of observations in some categories makes visual interpretation difficult. Looking down a diagonal from box A,A to E,E, however, reveals how the modal class of the distribution changes from A to E. As might be expected, the less convinced respondents are of the importance of reducing inflation, and the more they doubt that inflation is a monetary phenomenon, the more strongly do they disagree with a money growth rule.

# TEN

# The Influence of Economic Doctrine

The discussion of Section 9 proceeded on the simple assumption that views on policy might be determined both by normative attitudes (what should policy be trying to achieve?) and positive analysis (what effects will this or that policy have?). As we have seen, statistical connections between propositions can be observed which appear to confirm the influence of both positive and normative factors. Inspection of the data, however, reveals other curious features. In principle there is no reason to expect close associations between opinions on purely positive issues and opinions about policy objectives. For example, whether a person thinks that inflation is or is not caused by excessive money supply growth might be expected not to influence whether the same person believes that conquering inflation ought to be the highest priority of macro-economic policy. Similarly, whether or not a person thinks that minimum wage legislation will result in unemployment might be considered not relevant to the question of whether he or she is in favour of a more equal distribution of income.

As a philosophical proposition, the logical independence of purely scientific statements from normative judgements may be accepted, but as an empirical description of the state of economic opinion in the UK it is false. Agreement to the proposition that minimum wages increase unemployment (No. 1) is inversely related to the desire to see a more equal distribution of income (No. 29). The correlation coefficient between response `scores' for the two propositions is about 0·39 and is significantly different from zero at the 1% level. Only for three other propositions are the responses to proposition 1 more highly correlated than they are to proposition 29. The association can clearly be discerned in Figure 17 with respondents falling predominantly into the top left-hand portion of the figure. Most respondents in the D and E columns are in the A and B rows, and most of the respondents in the D and E rows are in the A and B columns.

Similarly, agreement to the proposition that inflation is a monetary phenomenon is positively related to a desire to see the elimination of inflation as the priority of policy. The correlation coefficient is 0·43 and is among the highest of those produced by our analysis. A glance at Figure 18 confirms that the bottom left-hand portion is relatively short of respondents, with a great preponderance of those in rows D and E also being located in columns D and E.

## 'Pure' and 'impure' value-judgements

This observation that associations exist between value-judgements and empirical propositions is, at a practical level, unlikely to occasion much surprise. An important point here is that value-judgements are often 'impure' or 'non-basic'—to use Sen's (1970) terminology (see Blaug, p. 133). A 'pure' or 'basic' value-judgement is one which holds under all conceivable circumstances. If there are circumstances which would lead a person to modify a value-judgement, then that is considered 'impure' or 'non-basic'. The value-judgements we have been considering would seem to fit into the latter category. For example, when respondents considered their responses to the proposition on the distribution of income, they would most likely have considered it in the light of their understanding of the practical consequences attending further redistribution. If a consequence of any further redistribution was a shrinking of national income to a small fraction of its present size, for instance, even the most egalitarian respondent might have been prepared to re-appraise his or her position. Similarly, the importance attached to an anti-inflation objective is likely to have depended to some extent on the respondent's assessment of the consequences of pursuing it. The inverse correlation between support for income distribution and agreement that a minimum wage increases unemployment might therefore be explained by invoking the influence of an empirical proposition on an impure value-judgement.

It must be admitted, however, that the connection between the two propositions is somewhat indirect. There is no reason to suppose that respondents assumed the only mechanism available for achieving a change in the distribution of income was via a minimum wage. To the extent that alternative possible policies were recognised, the association between opinions about the conse-quences of a minimum wage and the desirability of income redistribution would be weakened. Further, inspection of the correlation matrix revealed other associations between prop-ositions with no *a priori* connection. Agreement to proposition 1 on the impact of a minimum wage is positively correlated (0·44) with proposition 11 on the monetary basis of inflation. It seems that respondents who predict substantial effects from price signals (propositions 1 and 2) also see the money supply as the major cause of inflation (proposition 11), reducing inflation as the major objective of government (proposition 33), and further redistribution of income as undesirable (proposition 29).

The possibility that groups of individuals might reveal similar response patterns to a range of different propositions scattered across the questionnaire was investigated by Kearl in 1979. Using factor analysis, Kearl found correlated response patterns for groups of propositions which he associated with the 'Chicago School'.

'The factor as a whole reflects a political ideology as its dominant theme which only incidentally incorporates a particular theoretical position about the role of money in an economy.' (p. 35)

## A 'map' of high and low correlation propositions

Our own attempt to investigate this question uses a technique called 'multi-dimensional scaling analysis'. The aim is to produce a 'map' in which questions for which responses were highly correlated (either positively or negatively) and which are therefore 'closely related' appear relatively near each other, and questions for which response patterns were relatively uncorrelated appear distant from each other. An analogy (often used in texts on the scaling technique) is that of deriving a map of the relative positions of the towns and cities of the UK from a matrix of road distances between pairs of towns. The results for the 35 propositions can be seen in Figure 19. Only the relative positions of the propositions, as represented by dots on the 'map', have any interpretational significance.

As an aid to visual interpretation, two circles have been drawn around clusters of closely related propositions. The positions of these circles were determined informally by estimating 'by eye' the centre of a relatively dense 'cluster' of points and extending the radius until relatively large additions to the area of the circle did not appear to result in the incorporation of many extra points. On or within the boundaries of the two circles lie 18, i.e. just over one-half, of the propositions. A number of interesting features emerge from this analysis.

## An ideology of macro-economics

Consider first the propositions within circle A, of which there are 11. Circle A contains *no* positive micro-economic propositions and only three policy-related micro-economic propositions. These were

**Figure 19:**
**Two-dimensional 'map' of the 35 propositions,
produced by monotonic scaling**

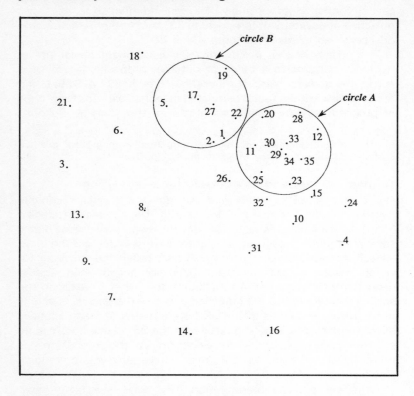

numbers 23 and 25 on the control of take-overs and the performance of financial markets, and number 20 on the efficiency of consumer protection. Each of these is near the circumference of the circle. Of the six propositions nearer the centre, all are macro-economic in nature, and five are normative propositions. Only two of the 11 propositions are among those we designated as 'positive'. Both of these (numbers 11 and 12) concern money: inflation as a monetary phenomenon, and the power of the central bank to control the rate of growth of the money supply.

Although our methods are not identical to the factor analysis used by Kearl *et al.*, the set of propositions circumscribed by circle A is representative of an ideology similar to the 'Chicago School', and our results can therefore be said to have affinities with those obtained in an earlier study. The circle centres on proposition 29—that the distribution of income should be more equal. Opposition to this proposition is correlated with a desire to cut government spending (proposition 34), hostility to wage-price controls (proposition 30), a desire to eliminate inflation (proposition 33), a belief that inflation is a monetary phenomenon and can be controlled by monetary means (propositions 11, 12, 28), distrust of consumer protection laws (proposition 20), and suspicion of government intervention in financial markets and industrial structure (propositions 23 and 25).

Of the propositions mentioned by Kearl as producing correlated response patterns, nine were included in our survey. Six of the nine appear in circle A. The three exceptions are proposition 26 on the power of trade unions which falls just outside circle A, proposition 10 on the stimulative effect of fiscal policy (as already seen, opposition to this proposition does not appear such an article of faith among British economists as it was for a certain school of American ones), and proposition 31 on the money growth rule (although other monetary propositions figure prominently in circle A, as noted above).

In general, it seems reasonable to argue that our evidence is consistent with a very similar grouping of propositions to that found in the United States, a grouping centred on a particular approach to macro-economic policy but also including propositions hostile to government intervention. Economists do reveal correlated attitudes across propositions which can be described loosely as ideologies.

## An ideology of micro-economics

If the attitudes to propositions in circle A represent an ideology of macro-economics, those associated with circle B are concerned with an ideology of micro-economics. Disagreement with income redistribution was at the centre of circle A. In contrast, the claims of economic efficiency are at the centre of circle B which lies midway between proposition 17 (cash payments are superior to transfers in kind) and proposition 27 (tariffs and import quotas reduce general economic welfare). The seven propositions in circle B are all micro-economic in nature. Three are positive (numbers 1, 2 and 5), and the rest concern the efficiency of particular policy instruments. Those who predict housing shortages from rent control, agricultural surpluses from price support, and unemployment from minimum wages are likely to be those who predict large efficiency losses from price distortions or other restrictions on trade. They therefore prefer cash to in-kind transfers (proposition 17), agree that trade restrictions reduce welfare (proposition 27), regard taxes as more efficient than standards in the control of pollution (proposition 19), and are prepared to accept the proposition that trade in human organs would be efficient (proposition 22).

The position of proposition 22 in our scaling analysis is of some interest. This proposition, more than any other, touched on the large issue of the suitable limits to market exchange. In every society there are differing beliefs about the morality of market contracting in various areas of life, and these ideas evolve over time. Medieval thinking was concerned about the morality of capital markets and interest in an age when lending would have been associated mainly with people in distress rather than with entrepreneurs keen to make a profit. In Jane Austen's *Mansfield Park*, Mary Crawford is a representative of the encroaching and destabilising influence of market principles on a conservative household. Mary Crawford is amazed that she cannot hire a cart to transport her harp from London. Indeed, she cannot understand the disapproval which greets her request simply because she happens to have chosen the height of the harvest season to make it.

'Guess my surprise, when I found I had been asking the most unreasonable, most impossible thing in the world, had offended all the farmers, all the labourers, all the hay in the parish . . . I shall understand all your ways in time; but coming down with the true London maxim, that everything is to be got with money, I was a little embarrassed at first by the sturdy independence of your country customs.'

Mary Crawford was only making a bid on what she assumed was the spot market in cart services. It is troubling to be told that at certain times this market simply does not exist. Carts or kidneys, the outrage occasioned by the implied questioning of long-established assumptions, the challenge to the belief that there are principles of morality that go beyond the mutual benefit of two independent contractors—these themes are at the centre of debates about the appropriate scope of market processes. It is not, therefore, unexpected that responses to proposition 22 are associated closely with a cluster of other micro-economic propositions involving attitudes to exchange.

## The role of 'doctrine'

The inclusion of proposition 22 in circle B draws attention to another significant characteristic of the scaling analysis. It is not the case that the propositions to which responses are closely correlated and which appear in the two circles are low-entropy propositions (those which produce relative agreement). It is the high-entropy propositions which tend to produce the most correlated responses. Taking the 10 propositions with the highest relative entropy (Figure 9 in Section 6 (B)), all but one are contained in circles A or B.

In contrast, of the 10 propositions with the lowest relative entropy, four are inside and six are outside the two circles. If we rank the propositions by relative entropy and compare the sums of the ranks of those propositions within the two circles with those propositions outside, it is found that the rank sums are significantly different at the 1% level. Our analysis involves subjective judgements about the size and positions of the two circles, but there would appear to be some support here for the idea that responses are most correlated across those propositions concerning which there is the greatest disagreement.

Perhaps this should not surprise us. We saw in Section 6 (D) that greater disagreement was associated with normative rather than with positive propositions, and it might be expected that responses to policy questions and normative judgements will be more systematically related to some underlying 'doctrine' than will be the case for purely predictive or factual statements.

# ELEVEN

# Ten-Point Summary

1. The survey reported in this *Research Monograph* is the first large-scale systematic attempt to investigate the opinions of UK economists since Sam Brittan's *Is There an Economic Consensus?* in 1973.

2. The sample of nearly 1,000 respondents is much larger than that achieved in previous surveys in the UK and other countries. It covers academic, business and government economists, and is sufficiently large to permit comparisons between these occupations.

3. Members of the three occupations were found to take notably different views on some of the issues raised in the survey. This was particularly so for macro-economic policy issues, such as the importance of a money supply target, the use of wage-price controls, and the redistribution of income.

4. Responses to the issues raised in the survey also varied systematically according to the personal characteristics of the respondents. Macro-economic policy issues highlighted differences between the attitudes of men and women economists, with women adopting a less 'monetarist' stance than men.

5. The survey reveals professional attitudes to issues of current topical interest. For example, the overall weight of opinion amongst respondents was against reductions in the level of government spending, was that replacement of domestic rates by the 'poll tax' will increase the price of private housing, that the European Monetary System is superior to a floating-exchange-rate régime, and was against the view that the prime concern of macro-economic policy should be to eliminate inflation.

6. Of the 35 economic propositions to which respondents were asked to express agreement or disagreement, some commanded high levels of consensus. There was substantial agreement, for example, on the effects of agricultural price

regulation in producing surpluses, on the stimulative impact of fiscal policy in a less-than-fully-employed economy, on the short-run trade-off between unemployment and inflation, on the legitimacy of the government's role in income distribution, and on the need to combine privatisation with measures to increase competition.

7. On the other hand, there were issues that provoked substantial disagreement amongst respondents. There were wide divergences of expressed opinion on, for example, the economic efficiency of permitting trade in human organs, the use of wage-price controls to control inflation, the importance of a money supply target, whether or not inflation is primarily a monetary phenomenon, and whether or not the power of the trade unions presents a significant economic problem.

8. The survey was designed along sufficiently similar lines to those done in recent years in the USA, Canada and several European countries to allow international comparisons of attitudes. There is evidence that UK economists are more strongly in agreement with a redistributive role for government, and have been less influenced by 'rational expectations' thinking, than those in other countries.

9. Evidence from the survey suggests that disagreement amongst economists on policy issues arises partly from differing positions on related 'positive' economic propositions, and partly from divergences of relevant 'ethical' standpoints.

10. The survey suggests the existence, as have earlier surveys, of recognisable economic 'doctrines', in both the macro-economic and micro-economic spheres. The propositions that give rise to high levels of disagreement are often those that serve to characterise these divergent doctrines.

# The Questionnaire

**May 1989**

**Dear Colleague**
### SURVEY OF UK ECONOMISTS 1989

We are contacting you to ask for your participation in a survey of professional economists in the United Kingdom. The purpose of the survey is to investigate the state of professional opinion concerning a variety of technical and policy issues. We hope that the responses will enable us:

(a) to identify those issues on which there is relative agreement and those on which there is disagreement,

(b) to discover whether opinion is systematically related to experience, area of specialisation and so forth,

(c) to compare the results for the U.K. with work of a similar nature recently undertaken in other countries,

(d) to examine whether there is a greater degree of consensus on technical questions than on questions of policy.

You will notice that, in line with similar work done elsewhere, the survey is "double-blind". We have no way of identifying any particular respondent, so your responses are completely confidential. This means, though, that we cannot send out reminders to those people who have not responded. We will be extremely grateful if you could spare the time within the next week or so to fill in the questionnaire and return it.

The first page of the questionnaire asks for some demographic information, after which you are asked to respond to a number of "propositions" on various aspects of economics. Please try to respond to each proposition, even if particular ones seem simplistic.

When you have filled in all your responses, please return the whole questionnaire in the FREEPOST envelope provided. If the pre-printed envelope has gone astray, you can return the questionnaire to the following FREEPOST address:

> Economists Survey
> FREEPOST MK1189
> Buckingham
> MK18 1XH

**Many thanks for your time and attention.**

## PERSONAL

1. Age  (please give age in completed years as at 1 June 1989)  ☐☐

2. Sex  (please tick the appropriate box)      male ☐           female ☐

3. Current employment  (please tick the appropriate box)

    Education ☐              Business ☐            Government ☐

    None of the above  ☐ (please specify) ................................................

4. Region of U.K.  (please write in the leading letters of the postcode for your place of work,  e.g. if the postcode is LS8 1JS, write in LS; if the postcode has just one leading letter, please write in the single letter, e.g. for B11 3PQ, write in B)

    ☐☐

5. Highest formal qualification in economics or econometrics  (please tick the appropriate box)

    Bachelor's degree ☐        Master's degree ☐          Doctorate ☐

    None of the above  ☐

6. Area of specialisation  (the categories below are the *Journal of Economic Literature* Classification System − please indicate up to 3 areas by writing 1 in the box you consider as your main specialisation, 2 in your second-choice box, etc)

    General economics; theory; history; systems                                      ☐
    Economic growth; development; planning; fluctuations                             ☐
    Quantitative economic methods and data                                           ☐
    Domestic monetary and fiscal theory and institutions                             ☐
    International economics                                                           ☐
    Administration; business finance; marketing; accounting                          ☐
    Industrial organisation; technological change; industry studies                  ☐
    Agriculture and natural resources                                                ☐
    Manpower; labour; population                                                      ☐
    Welfare programmes; consumer economics; urban and regional economics             ☐

## PROPOSITIONS

Please tick one box for each proposition:

A☐       B☐       C☐       D☐       E☐

Agree strongly    Agree with reservations    Neither agree nor disagree    Generally disagree    Disagree strongly

* 1.   A minimum wage increases unemployment among young and unskilled workers   A☐ B☐ C☐ D☐ E☐

* 2.   A ceiling on rents reduces the quantity and quality of housing available   A☐ B☐ C☐ D☐ E☐

* 3.   The fundamental cause of the rise in oil prices in the 1970s was the monopoly power of the Organisation of Petroleum Exporting Countries (OPEC)   A☐ B☐ C☐ D☐ E☐

  4.   Privatising hitherto publicly owned and operated industries will not reduce production costs unless combined with measures to increase competition   A☐ B☐ C☐ D☐ E☐

  5.   Regulating the price of agricultural products above competitive market levels results in surpluses   A☐ B☐ C☐ D☐ E☐

  6.   *Ceteris paribus*, a shift from a fault system to "no fault" divorce law will result in an increase in the quantity of divorce   A☐ B☐ C☐ D☐ E☐

  7.   The regulatory authorities will ensure that prices are lower in the Gas and Telecommunication industries than they would have been in the absence of regulation   A☐ B☐ C☐ D☐ E☐

  8.   The fear of being taken over is a significant force leading managers to increase profits   A☐ B☐ C☐ D☐ E☐

  9.   Replacement of domestic rates by the Community charge will increase the price of owner-occupied housing   A☐ B☐ C☐ D☐ E☐

* 10.   Fiscal policy has a significant stimulative impact on a less than fully employed economy   A☐ B☐ C☐ D☐ E☐

* 11.   Inflation is primarily a monetary phenomenon   A☐ B☐ C☐ D☐ E☐

* 12.   The central bank has the capacity to achieve a constant rate of growth of the money supply if it is so desired   A☐ B☐ C☐ D☐ E☐

* 13.   In the short run, unemployment can be reduced by accepting an increase in the rate of inflation   A☐ B☐ C☐ D☐ E☐

  14.   Non-tariff barriers have a more significant influence on trade flows than tariff barriers   A☐ B☐ C☐ D☐ E☐

  15.   Government expenditure has a greater domestic stimulatory impact than equivalent tax reduction   A☐ B☐ C☐ D☐ E☐

continued overleaf ...

|   |     |                                                                                                                      |   |   |   |   |   |
|---|-----|----------------------------------------------------------------------------------------------------------------------|---|---|---|---|---|
|   | 16. | The long-run consequences of financing government expenditure by taxation are the same as financing it by borrowing | A☐ | B☐ | C☐ | D☐ | E☐ |
| ✱ | 17. | Cash payments are superior to transfers-in-kind | A☐ | B☐ | C☐ | D☐ | E☐ |
| ✱ | 18. | The government should restructure the welfare system along lines of a "negative income tax" | A☐ | B☐ | C☐ | D☐ | E☐ |
| ✱ | 19. | Effluent taxes represent a better approach to pollution control than imposition of pollution ceilings | A☐ | B☐ | C☐ | D☐ | E☐ |
| ✱ | 20. | "Consumer protection" laws generally reduce economic efficiency | A☐ | B☐ | C☐ | D☐ | E☐ |
|   | 21. | Deficiency payments are more efficient instruments of agricultural support than intervention buying | A☐ | B☐ | C☐ | D☐ | E☐ |
|   | 22. | Permitting trade in human organs for transplant purposes would be economically efficient | A☐ | B☐ | C☐ | D☐ | E☐ |
|   | 23. | The government should take stronger powers to control takeover activities | A☐ | B☐ | C☐ | D☐ | E☐ |
| ✱ | 24. | Antitrust laws should be used vigorously to reduce monopoly power from its current level | A☐ | B☐ | C☐ | D☐ | E☐ |
|   | 25. | Financial markets are inefficient because short-term returns are the dominant influence, and long-term consequences are relatively neglected | A☐ | B☐ | C☐ | D☐ | E☐ |
| ✱ | 26. | The power of the trade unions is not a significant economic problem | A☐ | B☐ | C☐ | D☐ | E☐ |
| ✱ | 27. | Tariffs and import quotas reduce general economic welfare | A☐ | B☐ | C☐ | D☐ | E☐ |
| ✱ | 28. | The money supply is a more important target than interest rates for monetary policy | A☐ | B☐ | C☐ | D☐ | E☐ |
| ✱ | 29. | The distribution of income in the developed industrial nations should be more equal | A☐ | B☐ | C☐ | D☐ | E☐ |
| ✱ | 30. | Wage–price controls should be used to control inflation | A☐ | B☐ | C☐ | D☐ | E☐ |
| ✱ | 31. | The central bank should be instructed to increase the money supply at a fixed rate | A☐ | B☐ | C☐ | D☐ | E☐ |
|   | 32. | The European Monetary System offers a superior mechanism to a regime of floating exchange rates | A☐ | B☐ | C☐ | D☐ | E☐ |
|   | 33. | The prime concern of macro economic policy should be to eliminate inflation | A☐ | B☐ | C☐ | D☐ | E☐ |
| ✱ | 34. | The level of government spending should be reduced (disregarding expenditures for stabilisation) | A☐ | B☐ | C☐ | D☐ | E☐ |
| ✱ | 35. | The redistribution of income in the developed industrial nations is a legitimate task for the government | A☐ | B☐ | C☐ | D☐ | E☐ |

Thank you for taking part in this survey.
Please return the whole questionnaire in the Freepost envelope that was sent with it.

# Rankings of the 35 propositions produced by different 'disagreement' measures

The first Table in this Appendix (p. 93) shows the rankings of the 35 propositions according to three possible ways of calculating relative entropy from the response patterns, and according to standard deviations of response 'scores'. The rankings are all based on the results of the present study. The lowest relative entropy value, or standard deviation, is given rank 1, the next lowest rank 2, and so on.

The 5-category relative entropy values were calculated using the five distinct response categories (A to E) available to respondents, and are the values used in the main body of the text (e.g. Figure 9). The 4-category relative entropy values were calculated after combining categories D and E (the two 'disagree' categories), and the 3-category values after combining A and B (the two 'agree' categories), as well as combining D and E. Standard deviation was calculated in the usual way, scoring each 'agree strongly' response as +2, each 'agree with reservations' as +1, 'neither agree nor disagree' as 0, 'generally disagree' as −1, and 'disagree strongly' as −2.

## The Calculation of Relative Entropy

As in earlier surveys of this type, we have used relative entropy as a measure of disagreement or divergence amongst respondents. The calculation of relative entropy proceeds as follows. Suppose that $r$ response categories are available to respondents, and that the proportions of respondents who opt for each of the response categories are $p_1, p_2, \ldots, p_r$. The 'observed' entropy of this response pattern is:

$$- \Sigma (p_i \log(p_i)), \text{ with the summation from } i = 1 \text{ to } r.$$

The maximum possible entropy in these circumstances is when $p_i = 1/r$ for all $i$ (i.e. when respondents are distributed in equal

| | Ranking according to: | | | |
|---|---|---|---|---|
| Proposition | 5-category relative entropy | 4-category relative entropy | 3-category relative entropy | Standard deviation |
| 1 | 17 | 19 | 10 | 27 |
| 2 | 10 | 14 | 5 | 18 |
| 3 | 13 | 20 | 9 | 22 |
| 4 | 6 | 12 | 4 | 15 |
| 5 | 1 | 1 | 1 | 1 |
| 6 | 14 | 27 | 22 | 8 |
| 7 | 21 | 28 | 33 | 12 |
| 8 | 12 | 17 | 26 | 6 |
| 9 | 25 | 34 | 28 | 19 |
| 10 | 2 | 9 | 3 | 2 |
| 11 | 33 | 22 | 31 | 32 |
| 12 | 15 | 3 | 14 | 24 |
| 13 | 3 | 8 | 6 | 4 |
| 14 | 5 | 13 | 18 | 3 |
| 15 | 7 | 15 | 7 | 7 |
| 16 | 11 | 2 | 11 | 11 |
| 17 | 20 | 29 | 23 | 13 |
| 18 | 16 | 24 | 12 | 17 |
| 19 | 30 | 32 | 25 | 31 |
| 20 | 24 | 6 | 24 | 21 |
| 21 | 8 | 18 | 17 | 5 |
| 22 | 35 | 23 | 35 | 34 |
| 23 | 29 | 35 | 30 | 26 |
| 24 | 19 | 31 | 19 | 16 |
| 25 | 27 | 30 | 20 | 29 |
| 26 | 31 | 25 | 32 | 30 |
| 27 | 9 | 16 | 8 | 10 |
| 28 | 32 | 21 | 34 | 25 |
| 29 | 22 | 33 | 13 | 23 |
| 30 | 34 | 11 | 29 | 35 |
| 31 | 23 | 7 | 27 | 14 |
| 32 | 18 | 26 | 16 | 20 |
| 33 | 26 | 5 | 21 | 28 |
| 34 | 28 | 4 | 15 | 33 |
| 35 | 4 | 10 | 2 | 9 |

proportions over all $r$ response categories). The entropy is then simply:

$$- \log(1/r).$$

Relative entropy is 'observed' entropy divided by maximum possible entropy (then multiplied by 100 to express it as a percentage):

$$\frac{100 \; \Sigma \, (p_i \, \log(p_i))}{\log(1/r)}$$

For example, suppose 1,000 respondents distribute their responses over 5 response categories as follows: 200, 400, 150, 150, 100. The entropy of this pattern is:

$$- (0.2 \, \log(0.2) + 0.4 \, \log(0.4) + 0.15 \, \log(0.15) + 0.15 \, \log (0.15) + 0.1 \, \log(0.1)) = 0.646$$

(taking logarithms to base 10). The maximum possible entropy is:

$$- \log(0.2) = 0.699$$

so the relative entropy of this response pattern is:

$$100 \times 0.646 \, / \, 0.699 = 92.4\%.$$


## Correlations between different 'disagreement' measures

The second Table shows rank correlations between the four different measures of 'disagreement' detailed on the previous page. The figures in the Table are Spearman rank correlation coefficents, based on the above rankings.

| | 4-category entropy | 3-category entropy | Standard deviation |
|---|---|---|---|
| 5-category entropy | 0.42** | 0.83*** | 0.88*** |
| 4-category entropy | | 0.46** | 0.27 |
| 3-category entropy | | | 0.52** |

** Statistically significantly different from 0 beyond the 1% significance level (one-sided test).
*** Statistically significantly different from 0 beyond the 0·1% significance level (one-sided test).

## Correlations between 'disagreement' in different countries

The Table below shows rank correlations between the relative entropy scores from surveys done in seven countries of Europe and North America, based on the 20 propositions common to all the studies (see main text, Sections 4 and 6 (C), and Appendix 1 for details). The UK relative entropy scores from which the correlations were calculated are the 5-category scores from this study. Relative entropy scores for the other countries were taken from Block and Walker (1988). The figures in the Table are Spearman rank correlation coefficients.

|         | U.S. | Canada | France | Germany | Austria | Switzerland |
|---------|------|--------|--------|---------|---------|-------------|
| U.K.    | 0.25 | 0.30   | 0.18   | 0.11    | 0.06    | - 0.18      |
| U.S.    |      | 0.92***| 0.04   | 0.39*   | 0.42*   | 0.27        |
| Canada  |      |        | - 0.01 | 0.42*   | 0.44*   | 0.18        |
| France  |      |        |        | 0.27    | 0.32    | 0.25        |
| Germany |      |        |        |         | 0.70*** | 0.49*       |
| Austria |      |        |        |         |         | 0.17        |

* Statistically significantly different from 0 beyond the 5% level of significance (one-sided test).
*** Statistically significantly different from 0 beyond the 0·1% level of significance (one-sided test).

---

# Table A1:
# Policy Judgements and Value Judgements—
# The Case of Wage-Price Controls

---

*Cross-tabulation of proposition 30 by proposition 29, for those respondents who 'agree strongly' that a minimum wage increases unemployment (proposition 1)*

| Wage-price controls should be used to control inflation (30) | | The distribution of income in the developed industrial nations should be more equal (29) | | | | |
|---|---|---|---|---|---|---|
| | | Agree strongly | Agree with reservations | Neither agree nor disagree | Generally disagree | Disagree strongly |
| | 195 (100%) | 28 14% | 48 25% | 52 27% | 42 22% | 25 13% |
| Agree strongly | 8 (100%) | 6 75% | 1 13% | 0 0% | 0 0% | 1 13% |
| Agree with reservations | 14 (100%) | 5 36% | 7 50% | 2 14% | 0 0% | 0 0% |
| Neither agree nor disagree | 13 (100%) | 4 31% | 5 38% | 3 23% | 1 8% | 0 0% |
| Generally disagree | 63 (100%) | 5 8% | 22 35% | 18 29% | 18 29% | 0 0% |
| Disagree strongly | 97 (100%) | 8 8% | 13 13% | 29 30% | 23 24% | 24 25% |

Notes: Percentages are calculated across rows, and may not sum exactly to 100% because of rounding. The Table omits those respondents who failed to tick a response category for either proposition 29 or proposition 30.

A chi-squared test of independence between rows and columns gives a chi-squared value of 77·8, which is statistically beyond the 0·1% significance level (16 degrees of freedom).

# Table A2:
# Policy Judgements and Empirical Judgements—
# The Case of Wage-Price Controls

*Cross-tabulation of proposition 30 by proposition 1, for those respondents who 'agree strongly' that the distribution of income in the developed industrial nations should be more equal (proposition 29)*

| Wage-price controls should be used to control inflation (30) | | A minimum wage increases unemployment among young and unskilled workers (1) | | | | |
|---|---|---|---|---|---|---|
| | | Agree strongly | Agree with reservations | Neither agree nor disagree | Generally disagree | Disagree strongly |
| Base | 316 (100%) | 28 9% | 134 42% | 31 10% | 79 25% | 44 14% |
| Agree strongly | 38 (100%) | 6 16% | 11 29% | 3 8% | 11 29% | 7 18% |
| Agree with reservations | 143 (100%) | 5 3% | 63 44% | 11 8% | 43 30% | 21 15% |
| Neither agree nor disagree | 54 (100%) | 4 7% | 18 33% | 12 22% | 9 17% | 11 20% |
| Generally disagree | 56 (100%) | 5 9% | 35 63% | 3 5% | 11 20% | 2 4% |
| Disagree strongly | 25 (100%) | 8 32% | 7 28% | 2 8% | 5 20% | 3 12% |

Notes: Percentages are calculated across rows, and may not sum exactly to 100% because of rounding. The Table omits those respondents who failed to tick a response category for either proposition 1 or proposition 30.

A chi-squared test of independence between rows and columns gives a chi-squared value of 52·4, which is statistically beyond the 0·1% significance level (16 degrees of freedom).

# Table A3:
# Policy Judgements and Empirical Judgements—
# The Money Growth Rule

*Cross-tabulation of proposition 11 by proposition 31, for those respondents who 'agree strongly' or 'agree with reservations' that the prime concern of policy should be to eliminate inflation (proposition 33)*

| | | The central bank should be instructed to increase the money supply at a fixed rate (31) | | | | |
|---|---|---|---|---|---|---|
| Inflation is primarily a monetary phenomenon (11) | | Agree strongly | Agree with reservations | Neither agree nor disagree | Generally disagree | Disagree strongly |
| | Base 212 (100%) | 18 8% | 47 22% | 52 25% | 72 34% | 23 11% |
| Agree strongly | 58 (100%) | 14 24% | 19 33% | 4 7% | 13 22% | 8 14% |
| Agree with reservations | 90 (100%) | 4 4% | 18 20% | 26 29% | 34 38% | 8 9% |
| Neither agree nor disagree | 22 (100%) | 0 0% | 5 22% | 12 52% | 5 22% | 1 4% |
| Generally disagree | 34 (100%) | 0 0% | 4 12% | 9 26% | 19 56% | 2 6% |
| Disagree strongly | 7 (100%) | 0 0% | 1 14% | 1 14% | 1 14% | 4 57% |

Notes: Percentages are calculated across rows, and may not sum exactly to 100% because of rounding. The Table omits those respondents who failed to tick a response category for either proposition 11 or proposition 31.

A chi-squared test of independence between rows and columns gives a chi-squared value of 70·8, which is statistically beyond the 0·1% significance level (16 degrees of freedom).

# Table A4:
# Policy Judgements and Policy Objectives—
# The Money Growth Rule

*Cross-tabulation of proposition 33 by proposition 31, for those respondents who 'agree strongly' or 'agree with reservations' that inflation is a monetary phenomenon*

| The prime concern of macro-economic policy should be to eliminate inflation (33) | | The central bank should be instructed to increase the money supply at a fixed rate (31) | | | | |
|---|---|---|---|---|---|---|
| | | Agree strongly | Agree with reservations | Neither agree nor disagree | Generally disagree | Disagree strongly |
| | Base 407 | 27 | 86 | 106 | 140 | 48 |
| | (100%) | 7% | 21% | 26% | 34% | 12% |
| Agree strongly | 40 | 12 | 12 | 4 | 9 | 3 |
| | (100%) | 30% | 30% | 10% | 23% | 8% |
| Agree with reservations | 108 | 6 | 25 | 26 | 38 | 13 |
| | (100%) | 6% | 23% | 24% | 35% | 12% |
| Neither agree nor disagree | 73 | 3 | 15 | 25 | 24 | 6 |
| | (100%) | 4% | 21% | 34% | 33% | 8% |
| Generally disagree | 142 | 5 | 29 | 41 | 53 | 13 |
| | (100%) | 4% | 20% | 29% | 37% | 10% |
| Disagree strongly | 44 | 1 | 5 | 10 | 16 | 12 |
| | (100%) | 2% | 11% | 23% | 36% | 27% |

Notes: Percentages are calculated across rows, and may not sum exactly to 100% because of rounding. The Table omits those respondents who failed to tick a response category for either proposition 31 or proposition 33.

A chi-squared test of independence between rows and columns gives a chi-squared value of 60·4, which is statistically beyond the 0·1% significance level (16 degrees of freedom).

# References

Blaug, Mark (1980): *The Methodology of Economics*, Cambridge Surveys of Economic Literature, Cambridge University Press.

Block, W. and M. Walker (1988): 'Entropy in the Canadian Economics Profession: Sampling Consensus on the Major Issues', *Canadian Public Policy*, Vol. 14, No. 2, pp. 137-50.

Brittan, S. (1973): *Is There an Economic Consensus?*, London: Macmillan.

Coughlin, P. J. (1989): 'Economic policy advice and political preferences', *Public Choice*, Vol. 61, pp. 201-16.

Frey, B. S., W. W. Pommerehne, F. Schneider, and G. Gilbert (1984): 'Consensus and Dissension Among Economists: An Empirical Enquiry', *American Economic Review*, Vol. 74, No. 5, pp. 986-94.

Friedman, M. (1935): 'The Methodology of Positive Economics', reprinted in W. Breit and H. Hochman (eds.), *Readings in Microeconomics*, New York: Holt, Rinehart, Winston, 1968, pp. 23-47.

Hobbes, T. (1968): C. B. Macpherson (ed.), *Leviathan*, Pelican Classics, Harmondsworth: Penguin Books.

Kearl, J., C. Pope, G. Whiting, and L. Wimmer (1979): 'A Confusion of Economists?', *American Economic Review: Papers and Proceedings*, Vol. 69, No. 2, pp. 28-37.

McCloskey, D. N. (1983): 'The Rhetoric of Economics', *Journal of Economic Literature*, Vol. 21, No. 2, pp. 481-517.

Samuelson, P. (1959): 'What economists know', in D. Lerner (ed.), *The Human Meaning of the Social Sciences*, New York: Meridian.

Schultze, C. (1985): 'Microeconomic efficiency and nominal wage stickiness', *American Economic Review*, Vol. 75, pp. 1-15.

Sen, A. K. (1970): *Collective Choices and Social Welfare*, Edinburgh: Oliver and Boyd.

Sturges, Paul and Claire (eds.), *Who's Who in British Economics*, Aldershot, Hants.: Edward Elgar, 1990.

Thurow, L. (1986): *Dangerous Currents*, New York: Random House.

# IEA PUBLICATIONS
## Subscription Service

An annual subscription is the most convenient way to obtain our publications. Every title we produce in all our regular series will be sent to you immediately on publication and without further charge, representing a substantial saving.

### Individual subscription rates*

**Britain:**   £25·00 p.a. including postage.

£23·00 p.a. if paid by Banker's Order.

£15·00 p.a. to teachers and students who pay *personally*.

**Europe:**   £25·00 p.a. including postage.

**South America:**   £35·00 p.a. or equivalent.

**Other Countries:**   Rates on application. In most countries subscriptions are handled by local agents. Addresses are available from the IEA.

\* These rates are *not* available to companies or to institutions.

To:  The Treasurer, Institute of Economic Affairs,
2 Lord North Street, Westminster,
London SW1P 3LB

I should like to subscribe from .....................................

I enclose a cheque/postal order for:

☐ £25·00

☐ £15·00    I am a teacher/student at ...........................

.........................................................................

☐ Please send a Banker's Order form.

☐ Please send an invoice.

☐ Please charge my credit card:

Please tick    ☐ **VISA**   ☐ 🅰   ☐ **AMERICAN EXPRESS**   ☐ ◑

Card No: ☐☐☐☐☐☐☐☐☐☐☐☐☐☐☐☐

In addition I would like to purchase the following previously published titles:

.........................................................................

.........................................................................

Name ....................................................................

Address ................................................................

.........................................................................

...................................... Post Code ...............

⎫
⎬ BLOCK
⎭ LETTERS
PLEASE

Signed ............................................ Date ....................

RM45

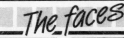